Planes of Being
Towards a Merged Mind

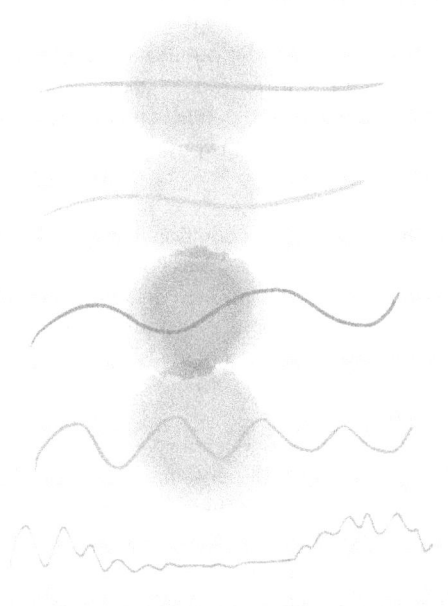

Planes of Being
Towards a Merged Mind
Third Edition 2015
First Published in Great Britain 2012

ISBN 978-1-849-14313-4

© Copyright Tom Evans

www.planesofbeing.com

All rights reserved. No part of this publication may be reproduced, stored in or introduced into a retrieval system, or transmitted, in any form, or by any means (electronic, mechanical, photocopying recording or otherwise) without the prior written permission of the publisher.

This book is sold subject to the condition that it shall not, by way of trade or otherwise, be lent, resold, hired out, or otherwise circulated without the publisher's prior consent in any form of binding or cover other than that in which it is published and without a similar condition including this condition being imposed on the subsequent purchaser.

The purpose of this book is to educate and entertain. The author and publisher of this book do not dispense medical or psychological advice. You should not use the techniques herein for treatment of any physical or medication issues without seeking the advice of a qualified medical practitioner. In the event you use any advice from this book, the author and publisher assume no responsibility for your actions.

Front cover artwork and various internal images by the author using the Paper FiftyThree and TouchDraw iPad apps.

Grungy Tarot images and graphics for spreads reproduced under license agreement from Digital N of Shutterstock.

Other images from Lucifor, artSILENSEcom, Boki of Fotolia.

In the Beginning

"What's the Point?"
wondered The Source.

The Mother of Numbers retorted,
"Let's get in Line."

"Let's make it Plane,"
decreed the King of Flatland.

The Queen of Cubes requested,
"Give me some Space."

"It's Time to move forward,"
urged the Knight of Karma.

"Turn over a new leaf,"
suggested the Page of Scribes.

"Fancy a bite of my apple?"
Eve asked Adam.

Contents

About this book	1
Notes for readers	7

Part 1 : Through the Illusion — 9
I : Behind The Veil	11
II : Thoughts from Higher Dimensions	19
III : A Brief History of Mind	31
IV : The Immaterial World	41
V : The Plane of Archetypes	51
VI : The Seeds of Creation	59
VII : The Formative Plane	67
VIII : The Material World	77
IX : Strangers in a Flatland	85
X : Signs and Symbols	93
XI : Leaving Cubeland	101

Part 11 : The Return to the Adytum — 109
XII : The Nascent Mind	111
XIII : The Flow of Thought	119
XIV : Plane Interaction	129
XV : Your Inner Oracle	135
XVI : Through the Veil	143
XVII : Lucid Awakening	151
XVIII : Even Greater Openness	157
XIX : Magical Living	163
XX : Beings of Karma	171
XXI : Deathless Reincarnation	179
XXII : The Merged Mind	187

Part 111 : After Words   199
XXIII : Keeping It Simple   203
XXIV : Spelling It Out   207
XXV : The Flavours of Thought   211
XXVI :The Essence of the Minor Arcana   217
XXVII : The Lost Arcana   223
Glossary   225

About this book

This book largely does not exist.

Ask any quantum physicist and they will tell you that this book is something like 0.0001% matter and that 99.9999% of the book, and you the reader, is empty space.

It gets stranger if you are reading this book on an ereader like a Kindle or iPad. The atoms of the device are again 99.9999% empty space. The ebook version of this book is even less real. It is merely a set of ones and zeroes stored in a file in a computer memory chip which again is mostly 'space'.

Only when the device is switched on do some of those digits change the patterns on the screen such that light reflects off it in different ways. The electronic version of the book is a simulacrum, or facsimile, of the so-called 'real book'.

Some of this light then enters the reader's eyes, gets converted back into electrical signals that travel from the retina to the rear of the reader's brain.

Remember that 99.9999% of the reader's brain is also empty space.

Somewhere on their travels, something much stranger again happens. The words in the book, which largely doesn't exist, started life as thought patterns in me, the writer. I picked them up from other books I read. Now you the reader are thinking something or other based on words that hardly exist in a book that hardly exists either.

Yet everything seems very, very real. If someone hit you over your head with the physical book, it would probably even hurt.

What is going on?

Some years ago, I was introduced to the Tarot. Before it was explained to me, I thought at best it was a con trick and, at worst, something akin to the Ouija Board and to be avoided at all costs.

After some years of study, I found that divination, or fortune telling, was actually one of its more trivial uses. While it has its place and great insight can be gained from a reading, even more wisdom and insight can be found from study of the structure of the Arcana themselves.

Like many things, the current Tarot has many years of interpretation applied to it by sages, seers and even charlatans down the ages. So I set about looking into the root ideas behind the decks.

This lead to me writing a contemporary interpretation of the Major Arcana called Flavours of Thought. The Recipes for Fresh Thinking that came from the Flavours are, in essence, modern day spells. Read them, incant them and 'real' world changes will come about as a result.

Like all magic tricks, they are only magic unless you know how it is done.

In this book, Planes of Being, my aim is to deconstruct and explain the true meaning and metaphors behind the Minor Arcana. Tarot buffs beware, this is not a book about spreads and readings.

It is all about taking the esoteric and making it exoteric. That it, making something unknown and hidden and transmuting it into being known, understood and usable in our so-called 'real' world.

You will also see how the Minor Arcana of the Tarot has been created to be a symbolic representation of how the Planes of Being interact and operate.

As I mentioned like many metaphors, such as much of the Bible, we forget about the original concepts of its creators and start to follow the sometimes distorted symbolism that has accrued over the ages.

For this reason, the mapping of the planes to the Arcana gives us a key to the practical interaction with the planes.

Rather than using the Tarot for pure divination or fortune telling, when seen as metaphor, we can also use it as an oracular source of wisdom.

Note that the subjects covered in this book, like the book itself, are by their nature both ethereal and intangible. If indeed they can be given the attribute of having a 'nature' in the first place as we understand the word.

The first half of the book is designed to open the readers minds to the possibility that our material world is not all that exists and that it is a convincing and pervasive illusion.

In order to ground these esoteric themes, the second half of the book aims to show how they can be used practically for 'real world' use.

If therefore they are not real but using them in our imagination helps us in our existence, it is a good thing.

If they prove to be real, this is also a good thing.

When I first had the idea for this book, my aim was twofold.

Firstly, it is the natural sequel to my book, Flavours of Thought. In this book, I took the wisdom contained in the Major Arcana of the Tarot and deconstructed it so it could be both more easily grasped and used in modern day life.

The second aim was to take the metaphor of the Minor Arcana and perform a similar deconstruction and exposition. Note that each of the Planes of Being relates to one of the Suits in the Minor Arcana, and for that matter standard playing cards, as follows.

The Archetypal Plane corresponds to Wands, or Clubs. The Creative Plane maps to Cups, or Hearts. All that is embedded in the Formative Plane is described by the cards of Swords, or Spades. Finally our Physical Plane relates to Coins or Pentacles, or Diamonds. You will see how it's not overly important to remember the specific details of these mappings and how they relate to each card. The benefits to be had come from simply embracing the principles involved.

So this book is not about the Tarot. Rather it is inspired by the Tarot. That set of 78 cards is not just a tool for fortune telling. There is a message in the cards that tells us of a Bigger Picture.

In meditation, something has been revealed to me up front about the real purpose of this book. The secrets hidden in the cards show that we live in a world which is the tip of a multidimensional iceberg. In these days of shifting consciousness, many people use the term Ascension and describe a process whereby we may leave this three dimensional realm and rise up to a higher dimensional existence.

My understanding is that what is about to unfold is subtly different. We are on the cusp of a 'Descension' whereby the higher dimensions are coming down to Earth. There is no need to 'ascend' to Heaven, we can bring it down here. We are in Heaven already.

The purpose of writing this book is not merely to explain how we interact with the Planes of Being. It is to act a guide for how to 're-merge' with them so that they, and we, are not separate any more.

The last time humanity underwent a shift of this magnitude, we gained self-awareness. We are on the cusp of another shift.

The full implications of this shift are not completely clear at the time of writing.

It appears though that the Veil of Illusion is about to be lifted.

We are moving towards a new way of being and an upgrade to a Merged Mind.

Notes for readers

There are several conventions used in this book.

New or compound words like 'flought', or 'sustend' will be shown in single inverted commas - a 'flought' is a 'flavour of thought'. Where the meaning of something is subtly different from the word itself, it too will appear in single inverted commas.

Phrases like the Archetypal Plane are Purposely Capitalised as they are Things and Intelligences like You and Me. Some people even give them Names occasionally.

Where a word is hyphenated like 'thought-full', it is to create a subtle difference from the common use of the word 'thoughtful'.

The glossary at the end of the book is a handy guide to expand and summarise what is meant by such words and phrases.

Part 1:
Through the Illusion

1 : Behind The Veil

Let's take a journey of imagination.

Just imagine closing your eyes while continuing to read these words. The fact that we can so easily keep our eyes open while visualising what it is like to have them closed is simply remarkable, if you pause to think about it.

Now imagine you are reclining in a comfortable lounging chair while on a sandy beach with your feet sunk into warm, fine, white sand.

You are sipping a delicious fruit cocktail. It's deliciously cold and not too sweet or too sour. The fragrance of the leaves of mint on the top of the drink oddly remind you of your garden at home.

The sun is nearly right overhead but a mild and cooling sea breeze makes the temperature bearable. You can see the horizon clearly across the clear blue sea.

Behind you, the rhythmic sound of a steel band strikes up, disrupting your reverie.

In your mind's eye, now let the sound of the band disappear by rising above your reclining form. Go up in the air right above the tops of the palm trees and look down upon the scene and yourself. You are now up with the sea birds and are free to fly away to a quieter part of the island.

Let's just unpack what I did there and what you may have hopefully experienced.

In the classic storytelling style, I exercised and activated all your senses in the order of feeling, taste, smell, sight and sound. When this is done, the same nerve centres in our brain are activated as if we were actually there. When done really well in books, on TV and in the cinema, we really feel like we are there and we empathise with the actors, the sights we see and the sounds we hear.

There is something much more subtle going on though in this process.

Firstly, we should ask where the seed notion for writing these words came from in the first place, when my mind was elsewhere when out on a dog walk.

Next how did this notion crystallise in my mind?

Why did I use this story out of all the millions I could have used? I could have taken you to the Taj Mahal, a lively bar in Paris, the North Pole or even off planet to the Moon even though neither of us have been there ... unless you are one of those lucky twelve astronauts that is.

Next, how did the strategy emerge to use the visualisation above as a metaphor to describe the whole book?

This method of imparting knowledge adheres to the age old maxim of, "Tell them what you are going to tell them, then tell them and, at the end, tell them what you just told them".

Now go back to that beach and imagine you are really there again. Where do those feelings, tastes, smells, sights and sounds actually exist? Are they objective external agencies or internally generated thought forms?

What makes this even more uncanny is that idea that everything we see in the real world is largely 'no-thing'. Most of the atoms of matter we interact with to create feel, smell, taste, see and hear are 'space'. Yet if we hit our thumb with a hammer, it hurts or if we see a glorious sunset, it is a joy to the beholder. If we experience something even more abstract and ethereal, like falling in love, then the most exotic set of biochemical processes are kicked off in our body ... often making logic fly out of the window.

Notice what imagery is conjured up in your mind' eye, when you read a phrase like 'logic flying out of the window'.

While I mention it, where is your mind's eye anyway? We all 'know' we have one but no anatomical structure is known to be it.

The short answer to all of these questions is that we live in a physical world which is largely illusory while also being very, very real.

This Plane of Being we inhabit is underpinned by other realms which, in turn, are underpinned by others.

It is merely a persistent and very convincing illusion that the physical space around us is all that there is to our world.

Excuse me being a bit techie for a moment but that is my background. What follows I promise will be as technical as this book gets!

So, for starters, the hearing range for a normal adult human cuts off at around 15,000 Hertz (or cycles a second) so any high frequencies accessible to dogs, cetaceans and bats, for example, simply pass us by.

Likewise, our eyes cannot detect ultraviolet or infrared although our skin and organs will complain if we receive too much of either. Sunburn and cancers being the tell-tale signs we've over-exposed ourselves.

Our senses of smell and taste vary from person to person and from palate to palate. Some people have differing thresholds to pain.

We are fortunate too that our ingenuity has allowed us both to measure the limits of our senses and develop sensors and transducers to extend their reach and, as a result, our knowledge of the Physical Plane. For example, we have radio telescopes that can detect X-ray sources billions of light years away. It these full range of such sources of energy were detectable to us as humans, the night sky would be as bright as the day!

If you live in a modern urban society, every hour of every day your body is being bombarded with ultra high frequency radiation from TV channels, wireless internet routers and mobile phones. If your phone has a signal, what it picks up and decodes is passing through you right now.

Don't worry though, the levels are generally thought to be safe. Some people even claimed to receive the old amplitude modulated [AM] radio stations via fillings in their teeth. While this might sound like an urban myth, there is a scientific 'real world' explanation for how this can happen.

Our scientists, physicians and geneticists have developed an amazing understanding of this so called 'real world' yet some pretty fundamental questions remain unanswered. Such as, how I am able to think these up words; so I can type them; so you can read them and then have similar thoughts?

When you think about this it is a pretty amazing accomplishment for what the scientists now think of as a bunch of organised atoms from two of three generations of exploded stars - i.e. Us, all life forms and our home we call Mother Earth. If you read one of Shakespeare's plays, you are picking up on the Bard's thought forms a few hundred years after he had them and thinking similar thoughts to him (or whoever did write those plays).

This is telepathy, or thinking or feeling at a distance, by anyone's description.

The fundamental flaws in the conventional world view of how our consciousness works is this. Firstly, that the brain generates consciousness and therefore all thoughts must be what we think of as our own. Secondly, that all thought processes are sited in the brain.

Fortunately neuroscience is catching up with what many ancients knew instinctively. Our brains are as a much a receiver of thought as they are a generator. Furthermore, that we have mind centres all over our body that are actively engaged at generating and informing us about the world around us. Our language, as always, gives insight, or inner-sight, as to the true picture.

When our 'heart was not in it' or you wish you 'went along with your gut,' what was happening was that your ego-mind took the decision to override and overrule the information coming in from the other mind centres. This is a great shame and is why we always regret such moves. Our gut and heart minds actually operate a few seconds ahead of our conscious awareness and they are invariably right. From an evolutionary perspective, they have been around a lot longer than the consciousness generating parts of our brains. As such, they are smarter and more informed about what is going on around us on all levels.

Our self-awareness is almost the last output from the process of interacting with the world. It is also thought that collectively our self-awareness is what consensually generates the physical realm we interact with and engage with.

In addition to the Physical Plane, there are at least three other Planes we interact with. I will use the terms Archetypal, Creative and Formative throughout this book to describe them.

Now I should state clearly there are many more models than this one including those with 5, 7, 9 and an even infinite multitude of planes of existence. The three additional planes I am about to introduce are not 'real' in much the same sense that the Physical Plane is not really 'real'. What happens if we accept them as 'real' though is a deeper understanding and resonance in the physical world.

Interaction with these higher planes is the way to unleash what we think of as magic in our world.

Like all magic, note that it ceases to be magic once you know how the tricks are done. This book will lift the lid on some of the more widely accessible and safe forms of the art.

It should be noted that all models only serve to allow us to get our heads around abstract and 'unseeable' concepts. For example, even though I studied basic quantum physics and wave-particle duality at university, I still prefer to think of atoms and their nucleus and clouds of electrons as mini-Solar Systems.

Likewise, this model of four planes is only as useful as the realisations we can get from it in the 'real' world. As you will see however, once you acknowledge the potential existence of additional Planes of Being, you will begin to question how 'real' the so-called 'real world' is in the first place. It is almost as if the additional Planes respond to our acceptance of the possibility they may exist and begin to communicate with us.

The practical outcome of this shift in our thinking is not that we somehow get 'taken over' but that our lives in the 'real world' adopt a more magical quality. We become luckier, healthier and more fulfilled.

We awaken to a new level of awareness and life becomes easier and even more 'real'.

11 : Thoughts from Higher Dimensions

One of the side effects of inhabiting any dimensional layer is that you can 'see' what it must be like to live in a lower dimension yet only imagine and extrapolate what existence might look like in a higher plane.

To experience a wondrous journey of the imagination, I recommend you read an excellent book called "Flatland: A Romance of Many Dimensions".

It is a satirical novella by the English schoolmaster Edwin Abbott written back in 1884. It beautifully describes what it would be like to live in a world without an 'Up'.

Do a search on Google and you can either buy it in print or for your Kindle for very little or even find a free ebook to download.

I won't spoil where it ends.

Before we begin our journey across and inside the Planes of Being, I feel guided to share some 'off world' concepts in this chapter.

It is not meant to make your head hurt, just to stretch it a little.

Imagine a single line on a piece of paper. If you then draw a line at right angles to it, then another and another, you can easily see how you can draw a square or rectangle. Feel free to draw it now.

Imagine now making it into a drawing of a cube.

Even if you aren't good at drawing, as I am not, I am sure you have done this many times - perhaps doodling while bored in school lessons. The vast majority of us instinctively know how to do this. The more artistically gifted might add shade or colour or even capture perspective.

We never think about this but we can imagine, and create, three dimensional objects on a two dimensional surface.

Spend a few seconds looking at this diagram and try and just imagine it as a flat two dimensional drawing of three diamond shapes.

We actually have to make quite an effort to do this, as it keeps popping back into being a three dimensional cube in our 'eyes'.

If you imagine however that the image is of a two dimensional letter 'Y', bounded by lines around its outside, the notion of a cube disappears.

This simple phenomenon is of crucial importance and informs much about how we are 'hard-wired' for existence in this plane.

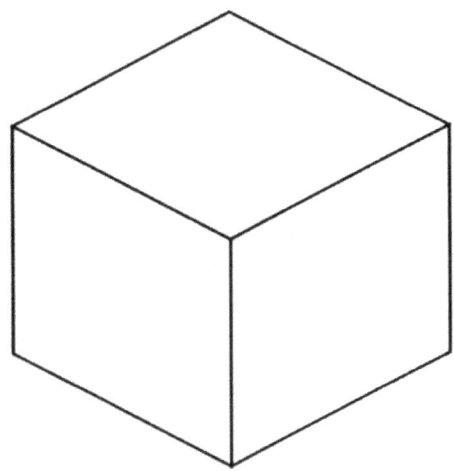

Now a line has length but cannot be given height without being connected by width. Note that a square is still two dimensional if it is horizontal or vertical because in two dimensions there is no vertical. We can only appreciate this subtlety as we are three dimensional beings looking at a two dimensional object.

Let's extrapolate a little.

Although we live in a three dimensional world, we are four dimensional beings with connections to higher planes. Don't worry too much about the latter statement for now, that will be explored and I hope explained.

As a four dimensional being, the fourth dimension being of time, there is no difference to the length, width and breath attributes. Apart from when under the pull of gravity, they have equal status as any astronaut will testify.

For the purposes of this discussion, we will also label these dimensions alternatively as odd and even. Note this is both relative and academic. So length will be odd, width even, height odd and time even … and so on. The point being that the even dimensions connect and the odd dimensions is where the 'action' is!

To a Flatlander in Abbott's book, the very concept of the odd dimension of height, or Up, can only be imagined and inferred. What the book takes poetic license over by way of entertainment value is, to a true two dimensional being, our fourth dimension of time could also only be imagined for them.

So in the same way the property of width enables length to connect with height, the property of time connects the three dimensional space with a fifth dimension. And so on.

Now if this any of this loses you, it is simply because of this.

A two dimensional being, if they exist, simply can't imagine a three dimensional world never mind a four dimensional world. In the same way, we can't readily conceive of what it's like to operate in five dimensions and above.

What we can do however is detect their presence by how they affect our three dimensional world and four dimensional time continuum.

If you imagine standing on a flat plane with your arms by your side but a couple of inches, or a few centimetres, from your body. To a two dimensional being, they would see two shapes you call your feet. If you were to sink down through that plane, your feet would turn to two circles, that is your legs, that get wider and wider until the plane intersected your torso. So at that point, they would merge into one shape but with two other strange blobs on either side that you would call your arms.

You sink down further and as you get to your neck, the oval shape of the body shrinks to a smaller, more circular shape before widening further out to the oval your skull.

Now if you are looking at this from a two dimensional perspective, you will not readily be able to work out a three dimensional intelligent being, called a human, just passed through your world. If you were inquiring and noticed it enough, you might be able to infer it. If the human crossed at an angle or lying down however, this would probably confuse more, rather than helping.

What is most confounding to our two dimensional observer is not having a higher level grasp of the connecting odd dimension of height which in turn connects the human to the time dimension.

If you aren't completely bewildered and lost, let's make another stretch. Imagine you are a fifth dimensional being. You will be able to see the time dimension as being similar to our width dimension. It merely connects the three dimensional being with all other instances of itself and its physical form past, present and future.

As time has a forward arrow for these 'poor' and trapped three dimensional creatures (i.e. Us), they can remember what has passed but can't 'see' the future or how everything is connected for them and all matter in their Universe. Some of them of course have a partial memory of some of the past events too.

To you as a fifth dimensional being, it is obvious. The three dimensional being however can get glimpses and sniffs of the higher dimensional worlds. In dreams and meditation, their sense of time distorts and can disappear completely to allow them to 'see' more of the whole. Much of the time it can make little or no sense.

In case you are getting confused by the way, the three dimensional beings are Us and we are imagining this for now from the perspective of a fifth dimensional being.

So, for example, when we experience light bulb moments, we can imagine that they may be nothing more or less than future memories leaking backwards in time.

Some 'tuned in' three dimensional beings are blessed with so-called "sixth senses".

There are six flavours of such super-sensibilities, namely:

- Clairvoyance - seeing

- Clairsentience - feeling

- Clairaudience - hearing

- Clairolfactory - smelling

- Clairgustatory - tasting

- Claircogniscence - knowing

And they are all examples of 'seeing' through the illusion we call our reality. I can also personally testify that they are not gifts conferred on a special (or crazy) few at birth. Every person has them innately and can develop them. Indeed most babies have these 'different-abilities' and they are tuned out as they grow, mature and are educated.

Note that this is not a bad thing, it is all part of being able to enjoy, experience and explore the joys of the material world we live in.

Children with their 'heads in the clouds' have almost literally not fully grounded. This incidentally is nothing some healthy cross crawling and mind mapping can't sort out, if you are a parent so afflicted.

Now I am a firm believer that there are no coincidences and it has literally 'occurred' to me while writing this last paragraph why they are even called "sixth senses". It is not just that we believe we have five senses either and they are somehow extra.

It occurs to me that these are the connecting senses to the sixth dimension and beyond. We will explore the significance of this later in the book.

Let's extrapolate some more. Let's give these fifth dimensional beings a label and some attributes. Let's imagine they are benevolent and they act as guides for us to help us on our path. If this is true, when they can't 'readily' incarnate physically or let's say some cosmic law says they shouldn't intervene, how would they communicate? By the way, if they do exist and weren't benevolent, we might not be around as they could so easily wreak havoc in our world.

Well, as they can see us right across our entire life span at one glance to them, they will be able to guide, nudge and cajole us into situations that would either help us learn or be in our best interest.

As we live on one of the few planets of free will, if we decide to ignore them, we can elect for a less than happy existence.

By far the best way to indirectly work with such guides is to notice and react positively to serendipitous, or chance, events. Then if adversity arises, to look at how we can learn from it. By simply assuming the world is not out to get us, a kinder world presents itself.

More direct communication however is possible. The writing of this chapter is one such example.

This chapter was not in my original mind map for the book. The seed for it was given to me in meditation just this morning and the information is channeling through me as I type.

Consciously I know I am going to finish this chapter by extending the concept of the fifth dimension into the ninth dimension but I do not know the detail as I type the very end of this sentence. I am simply being 'guided'. Note I am also open to the possibility all of this is a complex, psychological 'illusion'.

Our fifth dimensional being will similarly be able to detect that they too can sense and interact with entities at even higher dimensions.

In the same way, the fourth dimension we call "Time" links us to fifth dimensional intelligence, the sixth dimension interlinks the fifth and seventh dimensions.

This then is extended further for the seventh dimensional beings who are connected to their ninth dimensional 'guides' through an intervening eighth dimensional layer.

This sequence can of course go on but this is about as far as we can conjecture from our three dimensional reality.

Now from our position right down in our 'lowly' three dimensional world, we have been getting glimpses of the possibility that we are part of a wider panoply since we became self-aware. Incidentally, before we became self-aware we probably 'knew' all of this instinctively and intrinsically. We have just 'agreed' to forget it for reasons not readily obvious from our version of 'reality'.

Before the scientific revolution, which has given us an unparalleled understanding of the physical world, interactions with higher dimensional forms (and possibly extraterrestrial three dimensional beings) would be labelled as being a miraculous encounter of a religious nature.

As such, our kindly fifth dimensional beings have been given names like Ascended Masters. Seventh dimensional beings might be called Angels and ninth dimensional beings Archangels and so on.

Such hierarchies I suspect are constructs of our world. By the way, I only mention the angelic realms in passing as it may help you integrate all of this with your personal belief system.

At the same time, there are many scientists and mathematicians who are also busy researching the multi-dimensional nature of 'things'. It is more than fine for them to sit comfortably with the thought that the Universe has no such guiding intelligence. They conjecture that it is all just 'Number' and nothing more than a 'Blind Watchmaker' at work.

I do not profess to know how it all really works one way or the other. Like all these things though, I suspect the answers lie somewhere in the middle. This book takes an agnostic approach. I do hope and aim that this book is relevant to people at both ends of these sometimes opposite stances. As you will see, I am merely concerned with how we might use these ideas to extend our quality of life in this plane, not necessarily for us to 'ascend' up a level or three.

Having said all of that, I am not a betting man and I am not ruling anything out at this stage - especially when we are on the cusp of something potentially so transformational.

III : A Brief History of Mind

Most children are blessed with an innate ability to know when they are being lied to.

At an early age, I remember being told about how the world was made in just seven days and how it started at around 4004 BC. The adults stating these as facts had of course been lied to before but they both believed the lies and felt that it was 'right' to propagate them.

Nowadays, apart from some creationist fundamentalists, most people have a different view of how we came to be. Our scientific prowess has given us incredible abilities to allow us to correct the history books. We can radio date fossils and rocks back thousands of millions of years. We can interpolate backwards in time from astronomical data, such as the Doppler shift of receding galaxies, and theorise that the Universe must have come from a point source - called the Big Bang - 14 or so billion years ago.

It's a fair bet that these 'guestimates' are more accurate than the dogmatic answer I was given as a child from the Roman Catholic Catechism. What is more significant however is that they feel intuitively right. It feels 'right' that the Earth must be billions of years old.

If the Earth is that old, then what it came from must be an order of magnitude older. It is thought, for example, that the heavy elements that make rocky planets such as our home - and indeed Us - came from two generations of massive stars that exploded in supernovae and then coalesced to form new medium sized stars like our Sun. The debris and detritus left over then formed the planets of our Solar System - and countless others.

So if a massive star 'lives' for around 3 to 4 billion years and our Sun is their progeny, an age of the Universe of over 12 billion years 'feels' about right. How it started and what happened before it started is another matter and not necessarily the subject matter of this book.

Once our Solar System started cooling, it is postulated that primordial organic matter bombarded the inner rocky planets.

These organic compounds have a fabulous name of panspermia - you can think of them as 'star seeds'.

As the planets cooled, this panspermia is thought to have clumped together in a primordial broth and with enough time (and there was loads of it), some heat, a bit of water and the spark from the odd lightning bolt, some of it got organised into self-replicating molecules.

These molecules got more and more sophisticated and bacteria spread across the oceans and somehow morphed into cellular life. This cellular life got more complex and formed multi-cellular forms. These multi-cellular forms then evolved feelers and leg-type appendages. Specialist cells emerged that could detect light, sound and electrical fields. Some life just anchored itself to rocks and didn't move much.

Wind the whole evolutionary clock on a billion years or so and life had moved out of the oceans and on to land masses - and back again. Mosses became plants. Insect-type life forms had developed a different form of reproduction. Instead of cells asexually dividing, two sexes had arrived who both carried half of the code to make a new life form that came from an egg. The fish had worked out this trick too.

Another billion years passed within a blink of an eye, as nobody was actually counting in those days, and life had jumped up another notch or three. Reptiles ruled the earth and the sea. A complex food chain had evolved where one organism ate another all the down the chain, right down to plants.

Some plants even turned tables and learned how to entrap and eat insects. In the bowels of the Earth, nematode worms recycled the output from the whole process.

Add another billion years and mammals who cared for and nurtured their young gained a foothold - and arm-hold and tail-hold too. Instead of new life hatching in an external egg, it started inside the mother's womb.

In 'time', some of the mammals started to walk on two feet and then some even came down from the trees. These braver ones also learned how to make and fashion implements from sticks and rocks that they could throw from a distance to kill other animals while keeping out of danger.

They found working and living in groups was safer, although rival groups would often fight and kill each other for territory. The seeds of war had been born.

They even worked out how to control the way plants grew, that dogs made a fabulous burglar alarm and horses and cows were really good tractors. There was no stopping them now.

Come right up to the present day and I hope this 'Brief History of How We Got Here' makes some of sense. It's nothing short of amazing that, in a few sentences, I can describe a fairly plausible version of how we have come to be, hopefully without to much scientific jargon.

Note that I have extracted this version of events from a whole load of books from much more intelligent luminaries than me, such as Kitty Ferguson, Richard Dawkins, Stephen Hawkings and, before them, the likes of Darwin, Galileo and Newton. The full list of influences would be nearly endless and some of the more salient books I read in order to come to write these words are listed at the back of this one.

There is only one problem with this version of events and it is this. A large percentage of the technical detail is almost certainly about right but there is something intuitively missing - and significant.

To make sense of the world, we have to make assumptions. We assume the Sun will rise and set each day and we can even set our clocks by it for thousands of years into the future, such is our understanding of the material world. Well, let me disavow you of that notion for starters. The Sun remains pretty much where it is each day relative to the Earth and, as we all know but ignore, it is the Earth that rotates causing the illusion the Sun is rising and setting. Next time you see the Sun set, hold on tight and try and imagine the ground beneath your feet (and you) moving at around 1000 miles an hour away from the Sun. The Earth and you are also moving at just over 18 and half miles a second around the Sun.

Making somewhat bigger estimates like the age of the Universe also requires we make even gross assumptions. We have to assume that the so called Laws of Physics have been exactly the same since the beginning of time. For example, the calculations assume the mass of the electron and the speed of light have always been the same. Exceptions are made for the period of a few 'gazillionths' of a second after the Big Bang because the 'maths' doesn't add up.

Our modern day science is brilliant on the one hand. It has sent space probes to the edge of our Solar System and created technology like the iPad on which I am typing some of this book and perhaps the Kindle upon which you are reading it. Where science is often sadly lacking is in assuming that our whole Universe is a cold place where the conditions to make us, with our ability to ask where it came from, is a massive stroke of luck. Convenient 'thought play' postulates we are in one of a multitude of Universes, many of which are lifeless and therefore 'intelligent-less'. The reason we are here to ask "Why" is because we are here to ask "Why?" Using fancy names to describe this theory, such as the Local and Global Anthropic Principles, is lazy thinking no matter how plausible and attractive such theories might be.

To see the material Universe as cold and lifeless is sloppy and blinkered thinking. It's positively arrogant to imagine that all 'intelligent' life has to look like us, be carbon-based and actually inhabit our three dimensional space. Organisations, like SETI who search for extraterrestrial life, make gross assumptions life may use the same mathematics and communication technology as us and even have two arms, legs and eyes. On our own planet, examples such as star fish and octopi should give us enough clues that life doesn't have to look like us or share our geometry.

As a result of these assumptions, in our search for extraterrestrial life, we tend to look for planets that inhabit the so called "Goldilocks Zone" of temperature and single out those that have water, air and about the same gravity as Earth. There could be no possibility that some form of 'beings' can inhabit the scorching and acidic surface of Venus, the thin carbon dioxide atmosphere of Mars, the gaseous crushing gravity of the outer planets or even the heat of our own Sun. Now I am not saying that such 'life' does exist, merely that it cannot be discounted on a statistical survey of the characteristics of life on one planet - namely our Earth.

Looking back at our fossil records, we can work out roughly the size and shape of the brain of the creature from its skull. So we can see early man, did not have quite the same type of brain and postulate the frontal lobes - our thinking brain - were not quite as developed. Until early cave art appeared though some 200,000 years or so ago, we have no record what was going on inside the minds of our forebears. If we want to imagine what a dinosaur was thinking, we can find surviving examples like crocodiles or sharks and get some estimate of their level of intelligence and cognisance.

What we are sadly lacking is any fossil record of the history of the human mind.

By chance some years ago however, I came across a book called "Cosmic Memory" by Rudolph Steiner. I found that it had its source from an earlier book by Madame Blavatsky called "Remembering Isis". I read them and found them strangely intriguing. They awoke my Inner Child and piqued my curiosity, although some of the terminology is strange if not completely whacky. They described a version of events to explain how we came to be that at last felt intuitively right to me. I had done some past life regression a few years before I read them and one of the states of being described in Cosmic Memory was exactly what I felt I had been millions of years ago. At the time of course, I could make no sense of it and had dismissed it as imaginings - as you are free to do now with this whole treatise of course.

By their nature, their accounts are largely untestable and do not lead themselves to scientific analysis so they fall into the camp of mysticism.

Steiner and Blavatsky describe a more mythological version of events for our Solar System where discarnate, higher dimensional consciousness came first and the Sun and planets second. I will paraphrase the whole book in just a few sentences and suggest you read their accounts yourself as both books are magical in quality.

After the Sun ignited, its 'intelligence' nurtured the formation of the planets. As the planets formed, the 'intelligences' could 'hang out' on the planets and even shape their evolution. As the planets cooled and densified, so the 'intelligences' became able to take on more dense incarnate forms. As a result, on the special planet of Earth, and quite possibly others, the 'intelligences' became 'alive', first as the replicating molecules, next as single celled animals and so on. The molecule of DNA became a 'tuning fork' which could resonate between the material world and the higher dimensions. This whole sequence has lead to 'Us' and has almost certainly not finished yet.

Around a million or so years ago, we experienced a shift. Our brains gained self-awareness and then something even more magical happened. We learned how to take conscious control of one of our organs and modulate it with the thoughts we were 'thinking'. It was also around this time of course where our outer cortex grew in size. In short, we developed symbolic language and learned to talk.

Nowadays, we don't give our ability of the conscious control of our voice box a second thought, unless we have a sore throat perhaps.

What happened is miraculous in anyones' books. Some coalesced 'star dust' became self aware so the 'star dust' could look up at the stars and wonder where it came from. It could even share its self awareness with others so they could think what each other was thinking. This is of course a form telepathy. When we then learned a set of glyphs and signs to mirror our thoughts, the written words you are reading right now have the same ability to enable though transference.

Now even as I write this book, I realise its emphasis has already shifted from my original concept. I felt that a contemporary interpretation of the wisdom inside the Minor Arcana would be useful as a sequel to my treatment on the Major Arcana. I still feel it is and I will do my best to summarise it.

What is becoming clear however is that change is a constant and evolution takes occasional leaps and step changes. Human beings, all life and the Earth itself are on the cusp of another big shift. Such shifts are intrinsic to our nature and the fabric of space and time.

This time however instead of it happening to us as observers, we are in a position to steer, direct and even initiate it.

IV : The Immaterial World

To be a good scientist, you have to develop a deep understanding of the material plane.

To be a great scientist, you have to understand that our world of matter is the mere tip of a very large iceberg. You also need a really open mind - almost in a literal sense too!

For the record, I am not anti-science or against scientists. I am just not a fan of dogma of any kind. It is as absurd to think the material world is all there is as it is to think the world is flat, or that it started in 4004BC.

It is very understandable though why some scientists have become the new high priests of dogma. The underlying reason is because are blessed with two minds.

It's an urban myth and gross approximation that our left brains are the seat of logic and reason and our right brain, our creative centre. A more accurate description is that our left brain operates in space and time and 'generates' what we think of as our 'reality'. Our right brain 'sits' everywhere and 'everywhen' else. Note that even this is a big generalisation and not the same for all people.

So we can think of our left brains being generators of thought and our right brains as the receiver. To confuse things a little, it's thought our left brain contains a hologram of our right brain and vice versa. It is also known our neurology can be rewired in an instant, as yours is as you read this and mine is as I write it. This means the statements above can and do change. Indeed, as you will see as this book unfolds, we are capable of evolving to a new Whole Brain and indeed Whole Mind state anyway.

To be a good scientist, you have to study and understand aspects of the material plane in some depth, as I did when I got my degree in electronics and went on to be a broadcast engineer. As an end result of my education and first career, I know in some detail how light can be converted into electricity by a TV camera, encoded and sent over the airwaves and converted back to light again on a TV screen. This is the magic of 'tele-vision' and 'seeing at a distance'.

For me to have become such an expert in this televisual magic, my left brain was highly educated by a predominantly left brained education system.

I knew lots of stuff and to be such a good and sought after engineer, I was working predominantly with a highly developed left brain. I was incidentally fortunate to be also very inventive and created some amazingly innovative products from ideas that came out of 'thin air'. I only later found out how the right brain mediates this flow of ingenuity and how it can be encouraged and attuned.

So our education system is biased to generating left brained people. This has many benefits and has improved our standard of living incredibly. As a result, some people who are described as being dyslexic or dyspraxic often struggle at school. Some of these people are geniuses and actually possess different-abilities. Fortunately, many schools are now identifying them and helping them develop along different lines.

For some of our left brained scientists though, they are so entrenched in the material world, they cannot see their way out of it. Incidentally this is nothing some physical exercise such as cross crawling and some nostril breathing cannot ameliorate in a few sessions.

A good example of this happens when we do science on a quantum level, our consciousness not only affects but interacts with the results. Recently some scientists at CERN in Switzerland sent some neutrinos across the border to Italy and they arrived a little earlier than they should have.

This meant the speed of light was not the fixed, upper limit it was thought to be. If true, this would turn physics on its head and the rule books would have to be rewritten.

As happens in these circumstances, loads of other scientists whose positions, and even livelihoods, could be threatened if true, set about to repeat the experiment and got different results. A palpable sigh of relief could be felt rippling around the scientific community - Einstein was right. Well only sort of as the jury is still out.

Now I am not qualified to judge any of these findings but, as a fellow human being with an inquiring mind, I feel 'minded' to ask if such phenomenon occur or not depending on the collective belief sets of the experimenters.

So, if enough scientists think the speed of light is fixed, it will be.

Now I am not the first to postulate this and many scientists experimenting in the quantum realm are especially aware of such possibilities. I suggest reading The Field by Lynne McTaggart and The Science Delusion by Rupert Sheldrake if you want more thorough, erudite and entertaining discourses on this subject.

So by seeing the material world as all that there is and really studying it, we do indeed develop an amazing mastery over it - and this is a Good Thing. There is however a side effect to this. By taking this view, you quite literally close your mind and figuratively loose 'sight' of what is really going on. What I mean by this is the left brain becomes isolated and stranded in the material plane and cut off from the right brain which is connected to the higher planes and the collective mind.

What we lose 'sight' of is are the signs and shadows of the 'higher' planes in operation in our three dimensional world. This is much like the Flatlander who cannot conceive of the possibility of beings outside their closed world.

It's not just scientists who are prone to adopting this illusory position. Many politicians, the media in general and those who see money as their New God can also operate somewhat 'blindly'. Followers of most religions and even the harbingers of the so called New Age can be working with metaphorical cataracts clouding true vision too.

The delusion that causes this to occur is a result of us creating of 'things' in the physical world. By way of example, let me explain how and why I wrote the sequel to this book called Flavours of Thought and why this had lead me to write this tome in this manner on this subject. I should emphasise strongly that both this book and its prequel are both explorations not statements of fact. I hope it's becoming clear that what is true or false is merely a matter of perspective. Add another 'dimension' into any mix and worlds get turned upside down.

I came across Paul Foster Case's amazing book on the Tarot called "The Key to the Wisdom of Ages" some years ago. I literally vibrated as I read it as if I was being taken to another level of being. If you had to have just one book on a desert island or if you were incarcerated in prison, this would be it in my view. It lifts the lid on the true meaning encapsulated in each of the Major Arcana cards.

I found out the Tarot is not just a tool for divination and fortune telling. The 22 cards completely describe our very being and nature. Further study and understanding of their messages, then allow us to evolve into whole new states of being.

Incidentally, I found the cards can be arranged in a four dimensional geometric form known as a tesseract. As a result, a tool for evolutionary advancement popped into my world called the Cube of Karma. This was a pleasant and unexpected by-product of my research.

As brilliant as Paul Foster Case's masterpiece is, it suffers from two huge limitations. First it overtly mentions the word "Tarot" which is enough to put most of the planet off from reading it, which is a great shame as it is such a good book.

Secondly, it is a really hard book to read. I have read it over ten times and still have to understand it fully.

I did however get enough of the gist of it to be inspired to write a contemporary description of each Tarot card in my book, Flavours of Thought. I understood enough to know the 22 cards can be arranged in three rows of seven with the zero card, The Fool, at the top being the natural conclusion to 'everything'.

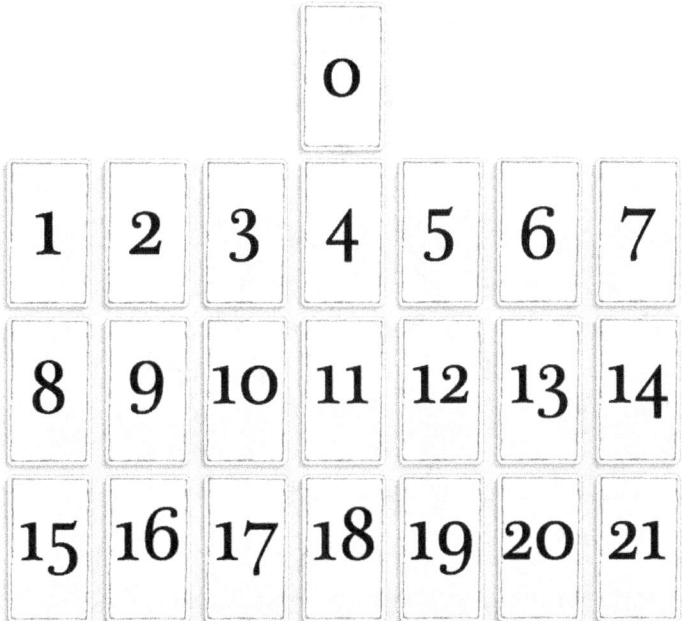

I also divined that if you apply the wisdom from one card, or flavour, from each row in sequence, you could get insight into many problems or opportunities. It was from here that the 21 initial recipes for fresh thinking sprang forth.

Note that I now know mathematically that there are many more permutations of these triplets of cards and they will lead me writing yet another sequel shortly.

Only in hindsight can I now see that Flavours of Thought, and hopefully this book, address the third and biggest problem with a metaphorical system like the Tarot. When we as humans make something manifest in the physical world, it immediately begins to be modified, improved and altered. For example, the ancestors of the Tarot are actually the 22 Hebrew Letters and systems like Myers Briggs classifications are its offspring. What happens is that we get hung up by the 'thing' and not its source.

For example, esotericists will argue about what order the 22 cards should be in and have endless debates about the minutest detail of a particular card. They start to debate the detail of the 'Chinese Whisper' itself and completely ignore the importance and significance of its root notion.

Accordingly in Flavours of Thought, the whole complex metaphor of a card like The Devil is encapsulated in the single word of "Perception". It is all the aspects of perception and what and how we perceive anything that merits real conjecture and analysis. Why The Devil is doing Mr Spock's Vulcan salute with his right hand can obfuscate not enlighten. By the way, this is not to say the position of his hand, and the association with Star Trek, is not worth investigation and study for those suitably minded. It is worth noting too that his role was to 'perceive' what his Earthling crew mates could not spot.

We know now that the matter of which we are made is mostly 'space'. This means the vast majority of what we see is immaterial. The material plane is important and its where we live. If something material hits you hard, it will hurt. If it hits you hard enough, it can even kill you. Note though that it was what lay beneath the iceberg, not its tip, that sank the Titanic.

You are of course free to keep your blinkers on but by learning what lies above and below our world that supports and even generates its very existence, a new level of being and enlightenment can be reached. It is entirely possible to communicate and utilise these worlds. In fact, we have all been doing it mostly unconsciously all of our lives. When we do it consciously however, a whole new cornucopia of opportunity comes our way.

As a guitar teacher once told me, "It's not the notes but the gaps between them."

V : The Plane of Archetypes

During the process of writing this book, my dreams and meditations have been delivering some new information and experiences.

This may come as no surprise as the material world takes a back seat when we are in the dream state. I am open to the possibility that what comes to us in these states might well be just be figments of our imagination. What is of crucial relevance here is that it is our imaginative ability itself that is by far the best tool to use to interact with any of the non-physical, higher planes.

As I write each chapter, I am mostly in a waking meditative and dream-like state anyway. The chapter titles themselves and the chapter order even differ from my original plan. During what we think of as our 'waking' day, the usual fears and concerns of a writer surface. I wonder if this 'stuff' in any good and perhaps if others writers have already done a better job in other books. As is the way with these things, when you tune in, examples from other writers that can help and influence you crop up all over the place.

At the back of my mind, I have had a nagging doubt of how I could do justice to this particular chapter. One of the qualities of the Archetypal Plane is that it is the most remote from our physical reality.

Its very essence is that it both unknowable and indescribable. We mainly interact with it through the intervening planes and its very existence can only be inferred - or imagined.

As is the way with these meanderings and a writing process mediated by meditation (if that's not too confusing a phrase), help comes in the most unexpected forms.

The first enlightenment came with the creation of the image below. I had seen it before when I researched the Cube of Space. It represents the archetypal 'plane' as a sphere in the centre. Note that a sphere is like a 'flatland' to a higher dimensional being. The Flat Earth Society have a point. This incidentally implies something may be in operation above the 'plane' of archetypes. Remember I wrote earlier that the planes may be infinite.

One way of seeing the planes is as stacked layers and I will explore that version of the model in later in the book as it is useful for idea generation and grounding.

In the version shown below, each of the three planes intersect the sphere and each other. The three planes are formation (left to right vertical), creation (front to back vertical) and material (left to right horizontal).

In your mind's eye, you can also imagine this structure sits nicely inside a cube. The resulting cube symbolises both our physical form and physical world.

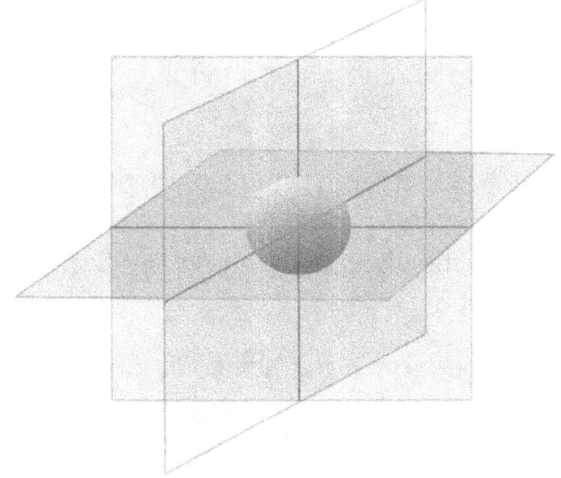

The second enlightenment I received was to be 'actually' taken into the Archetypal Plane itself and be shown what it is like 'first hand'.

In the gap between being asleep and being awake, there is a lovely, luxurious state of consciousness known as the hypnopompic state which was coined by the psychical researcher Frederic Myers.

I recommend each of us gets into the habit of stretching this out as long as possible, jobs and children allowing of course. The seeds to most of these chapters came to me in the manner which is why I prefer writing in the morning after waking and a subsequent meditation that elongates the state.

One morning a few weeks back, without any warning or prompting by me, I was taken into what I realised when I 'woke' could only be the Archetypal Plane. Note that the use of single 'quotes' throughout this book is to highlight and question our definitions and interpretation of the word so 'enclosed'.

The 'fact' I can remember the experience in some detail, without having taken any notes, is a testament to the vividness of the experience. I will paraphrase it here.

"I was in a purple swirling void. No form but with structure, almost like loads of interconnected neurons. The place, and I, knew everything but we also knew nothing. We had no experience but we had experienced everything."

"It felt like a comfortable place, someone was with me and I was then given a firm message delivered with some vehemence. It was also like I was in the centre of a star but it was cool and I wasn't burning. It also felt like home."

A voice 'spoke' to me.

"You have been here before Tom and you will be back here again - both for all time. We created the physical world so we could have 'experience'. Here there is none, merely existence. We took a lot of trouble to put 'You' on the earth plane. Go and immerse yourself in it and bring back what you learn."

The 'You' incidentally I took to mean All of Us not just me.

So the plane felt full of everything but also a void. The most overriding feeling was that it is the Source of Everything yet 'It' had a yearning for direct experience which it could not enjoy.

Without getting quasi-religious or evangelical about this, it was like we are the 'seeds' sent out to bring back tales of what we learn.

This model fits in both with the agnostic concept of a collective consciousness, or Zero Point Field, and the religious ideologies of there being a Creator and Source. To me, it is academic which is true and any debate is a waste of energy. Without being overly hedonistic about it, it seems we have been blessed with our time on Earth to go and fully experience life.

As the diagram above shows, we are 'sustended' (a compound word I made from sustained and suspended) by 'planes of being' above, below, outside and inside us.

By mere recognition of this model, we can then enhance and enrich our time on the earth plane. This is the overarching point and purpose of this book.

So if the Archetypal Plane is so ethereal and intangible, how do we interact with it? If it knows everything but nothing, how can we use it for practical purposes?

Again the diagram above tells the story. The Physical Plane has a direct connection to it.

In meditation, dreams and 'half sleep', when our conscious minds are quiescent, we can form that direct connection. For example, when we experience light bulb moments in our waking time, we momentarily forge a direct connection. The more you practise and experience both, the stronger the connection becomes.

Conversely, the more you run internal dialogue, especially listening to that 'inner critic' espousing thoughts of doubt, fear and scepticism, the weaker the ties become.

The Archetypal Plane is both the source of ideas and root thought notions and the receiver and repository of them once grounded and formed.

If you work in a creative role - whether an artist, writer or musician or a marketeer, copywriter or scientist - forging a connection with the plane of archetypes will reap unlimited and untold benefit.

Fortunately, we are hard wired for this connection. We don't have to sit cross legged in a cave for years or wait to be hit by a lightning bolt. We slip in and out of the meditative state naturally throughout the day. If you have ever driven home and not remembered the detail of the journey, you have experienced a form of meditative reverie.

Spending some time to learn how to meditate formally is time well spent. It is estimated that each minute spent in meditation adds at least a minute to your longevity. Work that one out and it's clear it's madness not to meditate.

Yoga, Tai Chi, Qi Gong and even just walking in nature are all forms of meditation. On my web sites and through my social media posts, you will find many links to audio recordings I give out freely to help us enter the meditative state and heightened levels of awareness.

I give them out freely because the scripts for them were given to me freely. I got them from the Archetypal Plane originally so we can all reconnect with it.

As we will see, this is all part of a Grand Plan. What goes around comes around.

VI : The Seeds of Creation

Inside a single seed are the complete instructions to grow a tree or a flower. External components are needed though in the form of soil, water and sunlight.

Occasionally, an external agency, in the form of a gardener, is involved in planting it in just the right location at the right time. Some intelligence agencies, like geneticists, even modify the instruction set to alter how the plant will grow.

You may have heard people talking about the Big Bang and the beginning of time. It is often thought to refer to a specific point in time many billions of years ago. Much research and thought goes into working out exactly when it occurred.

The 'when' is largely academic as linear time as we know it has not been fixed anyway. It forms around and from consciousness, not the other way around. The speed of consciousness also changes the speed of time.

The Big Bang really signifies the point from where the clock of time itself started ticking. Before that point no consciousness was around to observe it so there was no time. This wasn't so much of a bang either as there was no sound at this point either. It was more like the point at which the seed had germinated.

Time began when the Archetypal Plane spawned the Creative and Formative Planes from which then crystallised the Physical Plane, with its three dimensional geometry.

So the plane of creation is instrumental in both giving the plane of archetypes a mechanism to express itself and in facilitating the creation of space and time themselves.

It is not a remnant of some primaeval cataclysmic event. It is an active region and force, that pervades all matter. It also exists in its raw and initial form at the centre of all stars and, of course, black holes. It also pervades every cell, every molecule and every atom of our bodies.

You can say, "We are Creation and Creators." It is part of our DNA. We cannot help but to create things. Note too that destruction and death is part of the creative process as the old has to be taken away for the new to appear. The burning of grasslands is a good example. Another being how economic recessions are just the best time for entrepreneurs to spring forth with the next latest and greatest idea.

So the Archetypal Plane is like a sea of potentialities - a seething mass of ideas, concepts and wisdom. It is omniscient and all powerful. This of course is why so many people refer to it as God or the Creator. What ever It is and what you call 'It', 'It' did not and does not want people to worship It - especially just on a Sunday! This is like worshipping yourself, which is nonsensical if not simply a bit narcissistic.

The plane of creation emanates from the Archetypal Plane to allow ideas to shape into patterns. For ideas to manifest, they need a playground which is why the clock of time was initiated and space then formed around it.

If the 'why' is important to you, you can imagine there are an infinity of Universes - or multiverses - in existence and only this one had just the right conditions for events to unfold for Us to work this out.

When Time doesn't exist, you of course have an infinity of it to play with until you get things right.

If you have heard and been moved by a song and a singer, this is part of the process whereby you ears picked up the sound vibrations that were interpreted by your brain.

The Archetypal Plane holds all the ideas and seed notions of all songs. The Creative Plane contains the notions for all song forms such as ballads, sonatas, lullabies or rock and roll and grunge. It is almost like it holds the intent behind the feeling the song is to invoke in the singer and listener.

The Formative Plane will give each song its shape and the elements, like verse structure and melody, required to differentiate it from just being speech, a poem or simply a grunt, a shriek or a cry.

When the singer's mouth opens and their voice box modulates the air around them, the song which started as as seed notion in the Archetypal Plane ends up manifesting in the Physical Plane.

Nowadays, we can use devices to record and playback sounds we make. The seed ideas to create Edison's Phonograph and now the iPod, all emanated from the Archetypal Plane.

Now you may feel that this description of how ideas percolate through the planes seems to be somewhat academic and semantic. As this book unfolds, however, you will see how by assuming they exist, we can use them to create 'real' world outcomes. We can attune our consciousness to the 'vibration' of each plane at the appropriate time during a project.

So let's bring some of this esoteric thought into a 'real' world context.

Imagine you are in a business meeting to generate ideas for a new product. Someone comes up with a light bulb moment and everyone falls in love with it.

Excitement takes over and all current plans and products are thrown out of the window and the business puts all its energies, attention and resources into the new idea. This will save the business and change the world!

What can follow is for current business opportunities to be ignored as the new product is rushed into production with a few rough edges and snags.

Customers can then start getting disillusioned, employees start blaming each other and the old products may lose traction in the marketplace as a result.

What has happened is that an idea has come in from the Archetypal Plane and been implemented in Physical Plane without utilising the wisdom that can be gained from interacting with the Creative and Formative Planes.

Remember that, for the purposes of this book, we are assuming these planes are active forces and energies that we can tap into because they are an intrinsic part of our being.

We can use the energy of the Creative Plane to add more flesh to the idea by generating ideas for all the possible spin offs from the seed light bulb moments. If we do this before rushing into production, we see a bigger picture. Not only can we better assess the impact of implementation of the idea, one or more of the spin offs might be even better than the seed idea.

There is also something more subtle playing out silently right under our noses.

In the same way, that we are a product of the planes, the Earth, Moon and Sun are also made of the same 'stuff'.

The clockwork of our Solar System, and the Earth's path in it, are intertwined with the four planes.

This means that the timing of implementation of any idea is modified by the seasons, the phase of the Moon and the time of the day. One day astronomers and astrologers will compare notes and find they have much to share and learn from each other.

The fact I am writing this book in the Spring is no accident. All my books have 'sprung forward' at this time.

There is also a cycle that plays out over the years of our life span. It is also no accident that I was 49 years old when I started 'tuning in' and writing about this ancient wisdom. Every seven years one of our chakra points is initiated and it takes seven cycles of seven for us to 'awaken' - or not! Note that our chakras are often overlooked as being imaginary. They are actually active portal points inside, and even outside, our body that connect us with the planes. In many of us, they are dormant, atrophied or out of balance though.

So what we do by recognising that interaction with the Creative Plane is affected by daily, monthly, seasonal and annual cycles. When we align ourselves with cosmic forces, we go with the flow and make our lives easier.

We must also recognise the role of the Plane of Formation in the creative process and why bypassing it leads to us having to use more effort and rework ideas before they become fully formed and successful.

When we work with the planes, we stop pushing water uphill and start to live a more magical and charmed life.

VII : The Formative Plane

When we understand the role of the plane of formation and how it interacts with our daily existence, it starts to become clear how all the planes interoperate.

So the plane of archetypes contains all ideas and the plane of creation contains all patterns for these ideas. The plane of formation contains all the processes for the patterns to be brought into play in our world.

For a process to pan out in our three dimensional existence, it requires something else. It needs Time.

I mentioned before we can think of the plane of formation as being the 5th dimension, the Creative Plane being the 7th and the Archetypal Plane being the 9th ... and so on.

Between each plane is an even numbered plane that connects one to the other.

Now imagine if you were trying to explain all of this to a Flatlander. For starters, you will have lost them trying to explain what 'Up' is even like. It's obvious to us but alien to them. For them, this book might be a mystery at best and probably gobbledegook at worst.

For us, we might be able to comprehend the possibility of the existence of the higher planes from an intellectual perspective. As we haven't experienced the 'Ups' of these planes, we don't even have a language with which to describe them.

When it comes to the Formative Plane, however, we can begin to understand how it might operate and how we then can interact with it. In fact, we interact with it every second of our existence. When we begin to understand this, we can start to bend and manipulate time.

From our perspective, processes need time to be able to play out in our three spatial dimensions. If you were able to sit in the Formative Plane and observe, you will be able to see all points in time simultaneously for any particular process.

At the same time, you would be able to get an idea of how the similarity between various processes. You would be able to clearly see the repeated patterns across seemingly disparate processes. It would be obvious that they all have a start, an end, a mid point and various branches and even the odd 'blind alley'.

Only in the 7th dimension do you see how the seed patterns lead to all processes. Only from the 9th dimension, you can see how the seed ideas lead to the patterns which lead to the processes which in turn lead to their manifestation in the material plane. Everything in the web we call life is connected.

The agency which connects the 5th to 7th dimensions is light. In our mythology, the 'light bringer' Lucifer is thought to reside in the 6th dimensional layer. By the way, 'he' is not a devil, his role is to introduce and augur change. Religions, who abhor change as it makes control difficult, chose to demonise 'him'.

Right now this layer is particularly active as we shift in consciousness and awareness to a new way of being. The old industries of banking are crumbling because they have worked in the dark for so long. Light is the conduit for creative ideas to percolate into formation.

By light, this means any electromagnetic wave right across the whole spectrum. Light too does not just come from stars and light bulbs. Organic matter emits radiation constantly from cell to cell and neuron to neuron both inside our bodies and away from our bodies.

The 8th dimensional layer is something altogether more intangible but so obvious when you 'think' about it. Thoughts are the 'stuff' of the 8th

dimension. Every time you have a thought you are forging and breeching a connection between the 7th and 9th dimensions. This is why we think of the 'intelligence' of the 9th dimension as being omnipotent and omnipresent - because it is. It 'sees' and 'knows' all things, all at once. At the same time, it 'knows' and experiences nothing - or no-thing. It Just Is.

Thoughts from the 8th connecting dimension ride on **light** from the 6th dimension and get played out over time in the 4th dimension of **time**. The intervening odd dimensions are where 'activity' is carried out based on them.

Incidentally there is a big difference between those that are 'thought-full' and those that are 'thought-less'.

Both are engaged in the thinking process. It's just that the thought-full person is downloading thoughts from the 8th dimension. The thought-less person is wrapped up in internal dialogue, oblivious to and blocking out external thoughts from coming along.

Before I lose myself and the reader in a flight of linguistic and semantic fancy, let's bring this down to the 'real' world.

For 'things' to operate and remain in the Physical Plane, they require something to hold them together in not only Space but also in Time. Rupert Sheldrake calls this morphic resonance when referring to life but this force is more pervasive than that. All matter has some level of consciousness. Rocks, air, water and the chair I am sitting on all have a level of 'awareness'. If they didn't, they would not exist.

We are comprised of atoms and atoms are largely comprised of nothing - only about 0.0001% of an atom is thought to be something. That means we are largely nothing. The rest of the atom is possibility and probability. This in turn means we too are possibility and probability and that we can be anything and achieve anything we put our minds to.

The Formative Plane is unseen in our world yet it holds the pattern of each one of us - and all things. It holds the pattern for all instants of time for which that thing exists. It therefore is 'cogniscent' on a certain level of all things that have happened to that object in the past and that will happen to it in the future. It also can 'see' the interrelationships between the objects and how they play out. In the same way we can see the Flatlander can't see our 'Up', it can also 'see' that most people in this plane aren't aware that everything their life is pre-ordained.

For an incarnate being in our world, this leads to the illusion that we operate with Free Will. There is absolutely nothing wrong with this. If you choose, it can be a fun place to live and an exciting way to function.

The illusion of Free Will also gives rise to what we think of as invention and innovation. What is actually happening is that the present version of us is experiencing glimpses of future versions of us by interacting with the Formative Plane.

When da Vinci 'saw' helicopters and parachutes, he was tapping into the future. In these days of 'electrickery', we call them light bulb moments. Before the scientific revolution, they may have been described as Divine Revelations, Angelic Visitations or glimpses of the Creator.

When we accept Free Will as an illusion that can be transcended, a whole level of existence can be reached by imagining things are not quite as we see them. There are two aspects to this way of Being.

The first is to get into the 'State of Minds', where we can interact with the Formative Plane. This is known as the meditative state and is completely natural. We fall in and out of meditation with ease, as any car driver who can't remember how they actually got home can testify.

With very little practice that comes from a daily meditative routine, we start to enter into a meditative state with our eyes open. Indeed, I am in exactly this state now and I had no idea when I started this chapter what words I was about to write or where they would lead.

As this book is being written, it is already taking on a new flavour which may eventually lead me, and I hope the reader, to places and levels of enlightenment we did not know existed. If I was writing this from any other stance, I would be attempting to explain, or even justify egotistically, an existing level of understanding.

So when you operate from and in a meditative state, your thought forms take on a whole new character and our level of responsibility and ownership for what we are thinking changes at a fundamental level. We become observer and directors as opposed to actors and conduits between the planes. This is where the second aspect of this way of Being comes in.

By seeing things as 'arriving' as opposed to us turning up, we can start to see the patterns that are playing out in front of us. The numbers represented by the cards of the Minor Arcana are a metaphor for some of these patterns. For example, if you end up in the same unfulfilling job or disastrous relationship three times, it may dawn on us that something is wrong.

Just one eventuality we think of as us being careless and not trusting our gut. When we have had a sequence of two uncaring partners or bullying bosses, we may think that the world is out to get us. The third instance is an opportunity for us to get 'off the bus' and discover who has been driving it all along. It is and was always 'Us' - not the external influences or the system or the government. As any shaman will tell you, even climatic forces can be modified by our Will.

Interaction with the Formative Plane leads to a new level of existence and the potential for us to learn and invoke a whole range of new skills and powers. Indeed, one of the reasons it has remained obscure and hidden to us is that, in the wrong hands, havoc as well as good can be wreaked. This is why its very existence has been guarded by occultists and mystics. If governments or the military had any idea of its potential, in all probability, I wouldn't be here writing this book or you reading it.

Indeed remnants of past failures and experiments where interaction with the planes has gone awry percolate down via our mythology. The legends of Lemuria and Atlantis being those most commonly spoken about.

One theory that resonated with me was that evidence of at least one of these places cannot be found on Earth as the destruction played out on a planet between Mars and Jupiter that was destroyed which now forms the Asteroid Belt. The memory of these events is so strong that its embedded in our DNA and glimpses often emerge in past life regression. Such regression is of course another example of our ability when in meditation to see through our Illusion.

This means we must treat any interaction with the Formative Plane with respect and care. There is a certain amount of self-limitation in action and an external intelligence that will prevent us from too much harm. However it's advisable to be prudent and take baby steps.

For example, if control of the Formative Plane gives us dominion over time, the classic paradox of going back in time and killing your grandfather could be invoked. You might also 'see' forward by a week to get the Lottery Numbers. The plane naturally contains such flights of fancy. If it is not on your Life Path to win the Lottery, it's hard to see the numbers although you might see them in someone else's future timeline. The fact you are reading this means at no point in the future did you commit murder back in time.

More creative utilisations of the plane can be more easily devised. For example, if you are writing a book that will be published, you can tune into the 'future you' who knows the words that you haven't written yet. If you are harbouring an illness or disease, you can go back in time and heal the first time you picked up the affliction and thus heal yourself in the present.

Now there is nothing to prove if either of these examples are illusory. The only 'proof', should it be needed, is if such flights of the imagination lead to 'real' world results.

In my experience with many clients, they do. I have lost count of the number of troublesome ailments that have vapourised in just one session.

We have a couple of choices when it comes to working with the higher planes. We can embrace the possibility of the existence of other Planes of Being and learn how to live a charmed and magical life. Alternatively, we can elect to struggle.

As we possess Free Will, or the illusion of it, either path is yours to choose. Noting, in passing, that the choice of either path was also preordained.

VIII : The Material World

It is part of the way things work, and the 'Grand Design', that the Material World seems to us to be all that exists.

Our scientists have made great strides understanding and controlling it in fabulous detail. Humans have become Masters of the Material Domain.

Some of the bigger questions like why we came to be here, and became self-aware, and why so much matter is 'dark' remain unanswered. To find the answers to these conundrums, science would do well to embrace mysticism and allow metaphysics to give rise to some of the new the seed notions that give rise to the new physics. The smarter and more open scientists are on the case.

This does not mean throwing the baby our with the bath water.

It means that our minds have to be open to everything we see being an incredibly convincing illusion and a pervasive consensual reality.

When we accept this for all its implications, two new levels of possibility open up for us. Both require us to have our egos well in check, lest we cause havoc and become a cross between a bull in a china shop and a child in a sweet shop.

The first realisation is to embrace that we don't so much live in a Material World but in a 'Plane of Manifestation'. Here thoughts not only become things but are things. We can think and dream any flavour of reality into existence. Thought forms can become manifest. We are not slaves to external conditions but generators of the world we inhabit. Incidentally, this is true of all life forms to varying extents.

The second realisation is that we possess a powerful, yet mostly nascent and dormant, ability to tap into and utilise the forces residing in the other three planes.

This is not a new thing. All great strides forwards in the arts, humanities and sciences were made by a genius tapping into the higher planes. You could even redefine the word genius to describe anybody who possesses the ability to see through the illusion and to think and do something with their 'different-ability'.

The great philosophers and scientists such as Archimedes, Galileo, da Vinci and Newton were all reported to have had mystical experiences. Some of them were even practicing alchemists. There were many luminaries and mystics like Thomas Aquinas and Emmanuel Swedenborg who pursued and researched the metaphysical connection with more vigour.

In more recent and materialistic times, people like Thomas Edison, Henry Ford and Steve Jobs introduced 'disruptive' technology that challenged and changed the accepted paradigm. We now could not dream of not being able to switch on a light, drive a car or interact with the world through a tablet computer.

Religions have kept all the best the secrets known by mystics, sages and gurus from the masses.

I used to think this strategy was a bit of a conspiracy but I now suspect, in retrospect, it has probably been mostly to protect us. What is clear though is while our command and mastery of the material world has increased out of all recognition and imagination, our connection with the ethereal realms has atrophied somewhat.

Our resulting secular society is a testament to this but fortunately disaffection with the more gross excesses of our so-called modern world lead to some people seeking another way.

It is worth pointing out too that all the geniuses mentioned here and, in most discussions on this theme, are men. It is now time to allow the intuitive intelligence of the feminine energy to shine forth.

The secrets behind how to forge a bridge between the material and ethereal worlds are encoded in the Major and Minor Arcana and other glyphs. In the book Flavours of Thought, I show how each of our thoughts are modulated by one of 22 'intelligences' or root thought notions. Furthermore, it is important to note how the 21 of the intelligences are distributed into their three groups of seven, with the 22nd being 'The Obvious' or light bulb moment.

The Minor Arcana describes the activities of each of the planes which are described in these last few chapters. In order to now understand how to interact and manipulate the forces of the planes some understanding of the deck of cards is needed. I emphasise here that this is not a book about divination or 'reading the cards'. Neither does this book attempt to explain scientific mysteries as mentioned above.

I do hope though it is a signpost where to look for answers, if that is your 'thing'.

The Minor Arcana is divided into four suits and, as mentioned earlier, it is thought by some that these suits correspond to a standard pack of playing cards. For the purposes of this book, that's academic.

As a reminder, the correspondences are The Archetypal Plane corresponding to Wands, or Clubs. The Creative Plane maps to Cups, or Hearts. The Formative Plane is described by the cards of Swords, or Spades. Finally our Physical Plane and Material World relates to Coins or Pentacles, or somewhat appropriately Diamonds.

Each suit comprises of 10 numbered cards from Ace to Ten. As you will see, each number corresponds to an aspect of our being as our world is fabricated and 'sustended' by numbers. Each suit also contains four court cards, one more than the standard pack of playing cards.

These are the familiar King, Queen and Knight but with an additional card called the Page. They each correspond to our Spirit, our Soul, our Personal Energies and our Physical Body.

In total four suits of fourteen cards gives us 56 cards in total to 'play' with. We will deal with the significance of the numbers later but it an exploration of the significance of the court cards gives us some insight into our nature and what drives us.

So the King of Wands relates to idea, from the Archetypal Plane, of our Spirit. The Queen of Wands relates to the idea of our Soul. The Knight of Wands denotes the idea of our Energies and the Page of Wands to the idea of our Body.

The King, Queen, Knight and Page of Cups correspond to the patterns of Spirit, Soul, Energy and Body. The court cards of Swords relate to the processes of processes of Spirit, Soul, Energy and Body. Those of Pentacles relate to the actual manifestation of Spirit, Soul, Energy and Body in each of us.

What is of more importance here than the actual correspondences themselves is that we each have four aspects of our being which each can interact with the four planes.

Most people, of course, are unaware of this. Yet enlightenment can only come from a position of relative ignorance. Our bodies are like the tip of a huge iceberg and so much untapped potential is open to all of us.

If we look at healthcare for example, as masters of the physical domain, our doctors are expert at fixing what is broken. We can mend broken bones, re-graft burnt skin and even replace many organs. It is not common however for doctors to scan and heal the auric field described by the Knight of each suit. Conventional medicine would not countenance the possibility that an illness is something a soul may have been carrying across many lifetimes.

Our energetic field reflects our health and is a mirror of it. Much can be gleaned from working with it. I can testify that seeing and healing at the auric level is a latent skill we all possess.

It is not so much that we possess a body that generates an aura. A better description is that our body distils or crystallises from our aura and that our auric field 'sustends' the body.

When it decays and leaves the earth plane, our body dies - not the other way around. As the Hanged Man card so pictorially describes, virtually everything we take for granted is not as it seems.

Our Soul aspects as described by the Queen of each suit inform us of who we really are and what our purpose really is. Understanding our lives by looking at our soul's karmic mission allow us to evolve in leaps and bounds.

We can let old un-serving patterns go and define new ones going forward from a position of new understanding. The changes that result from such release make instant changes at a neurological level. I have seen people who release and void karma look younger and more vibrant. The health benefits of such increased vitality cannot be ignored.

The King of each suit defines the interaction of each plane of being with our Spirit. Here though a much more subtle interaction is in play. It is not so much that each plane somehow generates and forms our Spirit. Rather our Spirit and the Planes are an integral part of each other.

Real dominion over, and understanding of, the Material Plane require us to interact with the other planes.

The wisdom contained in the Minor Arcana shows how the planes operate and give us a system to utilise that invokes them into action.

IX : Strangers in a Flatland

Just imagine if you wanted to communicate with a person living in a Flatland.

For starters, you can't just wander up to them and say, "Hi". They wouldn't recognise your three dimensional form and your sounds will sound garbled to them, even if they could understand your language.

As a higher dimensional being, you would have to make allowance for their inability to comprehend many of the things you take for granted.

You would also have to be patient and come up with a system that was reliable enough to give meaningful information whilst also letting the Flatlander know that the communication was coming from outside their realm.

In the absence of a formal language, you might try numbers first. You would be aware that not all beings, or systems, use the same number base so you would use either trial and error or maybe even work out from the mathematics of their world what numbers would be significant to them. For example, they might count in base 2 for lines, three for triangles, four for rectangles and so on. Or they may worship the number six as representing the perfection of interlocking hexagons.

So if you wanted to catch someone's attention in Flatland, you might insert three fingers of your multidimensional hand in a certain pattern and with the same number of repeated insertions. The Flatlander would first spot something odd. For example, they may see three blobs come out of nowhere. 'Nowhere' being what we refer to as 'Up', of course. At first they may think that they were imagining it. You repeat the insertion and they pay attention.

If you were to do this the same time every day, they might bring their friends around to observe this strange phenomenon. Some of their friends might be Flatland scientists and mathematicians and use this occurrence to postulate the existence of higher dimensions. Others may worship the Three Blobs.

Somewhere else in Flatland, some people may have seen the insertion of four fingers and proclaim that their God of Four is mightier than a mere Angel of Three. It is all too easy to end up with the wrong conclusion when interpreting mystical and other worldly phenomena.

From the other perspective and without language, how would the Flatlander communicate back to us that they have seen us and recognise us?

Imagine you inserted your three fingers in the pattern of an equilateral triangle or four fingers in a straight line. If you saw three or four representative from Flatland split from the throng of onlookers and spread out to mirrored your shape, you would know that communication lines were open.

You could then start to change the patterns and even move your fingers around in order to create a pseudo language. You might even get really brave and slowly drop your whole body into and through Flatland, starting with your feet first and ending with you head, as described earlier. This would of course be confusing at first and perhaps may always remain a step too far for most Flatlanders.

Exactly the same types of issues exist for us when we want to interact with higher planes of being. For starters, any interaction falls into the camp of being strange at the least and possibly illusory and delusional at worst. While this whole book might be seen as a flight of fancy or the musings of a wild imagination, the seed behind writing it in the first place is that I started noticing and experiencing slightly weird phenomena in my mid-forties. The more I researched them, the more I found I wasn't alone. So at the very least, it is mass delusion and I am in good company.

I then found that metaphors such as the Major and Minor Arcana of the Tarot alluded to and described these other planes of existence. They were encoded in the cards even though many Tarot Readers have been ignored this relevance in favour of mere fortune telling at the end of a pier. Using the Tarot for this purpose, Paul Foster Case describes as being like sitting in a motor car without petrol, making engine noises and imagining you are driving somewhere.

Note, as this is not a book about reading the cards, I have listed the significance (and one of many interpretations) of the numbered cards of the Minor Arcana in the After Words at the back of this book.

The strange phenomena I started to experience did not fit into my previous model of the world. I am trained as an electronic engineer and have a good grasp of how the magic of 'electrickery' works. When I started to see past and future lives in peoples' auras, I did not have any ready explanation for this. I wondered if it was just imagination, and a flight of fancy, that I could teach authors to 'tune' into the words they had yet to write using simple hypnotic techniques.

What really did get my attention was the visitation by 'other worldly' entities, mainly at night, who seemed to be performing what I could only describe as 're-programming' on me.

The shapes and forms of these entities are as strange and unrecognisable to me as our three dimensional bodies are to a Flatlander. They did have patterns and colours though. Following such re-programmings, I began to 'know' things I didn't 'know' and to do things I didn't know I could do. The different-ability to 'see' and heal across time and space came to me.

As these changes occurred in me, they brought me into contact with others who had experienced similar, and sometimes more extreme, interactions. I played them down and have taken quite some years to step up to and own up to the abilities that came along as a result.

After some initial reluctance, I now find myself teaching and initiating others in some of the techniques I have learned. The jury is out on the what and the why but I do feel compelled at the very least to explore in the spirit of understanding why we are here. At no time incidentally, did I feel threatened by any of these visitations. They did come mixed with a fair amount of astral travelling and out of body experiences.

What kicked all of this off was my practice of regular daily meditation. I used to think that meditation is a waste of time and I had no idea how to make my active mind go quiet. Now I teach how to do it and how we can bend time and space by 'getting in the zone'.

Meditation has so many health benefits but one of its key secrets is that it allows us to see through the veil of our world into the planes of consciousness beyond.

When we are in a deep meditative state, we can connect directly to the plane of archetypes and seed ideas. To get to this state, we have to enter vipassanic meditation where we meditate on thoughts such they collapse in on themselves. In a lighter state, known as samathic meditation, where we tune into our breath or a mantra, we become naturally attuned to the Creative and Formative Planes. Only when we are wide awake, does the Physical Plane spring back into 'existence'.

With some little practice, we can learn to be in a meditative state with our eyes open and to see through the illusion of our 'reality'. This is how you can 'see' across space and time. I learned also that when I enter this state, it is relatively easy to get a client you are working with or attendees of a workshop to mirror and follow you. This is an example of how we consensually create our usual reality. There are 7 billion people all making this existence. Either individually or in a small group, we can change what we experience. This means we can change our world.

What I also discovered along the way is how to tap into the intelligence and energy of the cards in the Tarot.

Using the cards individually, or in groups, invokes that energy such that we can tune into and utilise it. When I concocted recipes for 'real world' issues and opportunities, like falling in love or making a decision, and found they worked. To all intents and purposes, they are like modern day spells or incantations.

What I suspect is really unfolding is that they give us a back door key to access other worldly aspects of our being.

X : Signs and Symbols

In order to understand the world and communicate to each other, we use a code called language.

So we all agree, for example, something is red and we call it "red". If it is similar to red, we call it "reddish" or if it is a lighter shade, we call it "pink". Naturally some colour blind people might have a slightly different view of the world.

Every so often, by consensual agreement, the meaning of words get flipped on their head. The Michael Jackson song "Bad" reflected, and influenced and even initiated, the use of the word 'bad' to refer to something that was rather good, or cool. More recently, things that are 'sick' are to be admired and idolised.

Such morphing of the language might send shivers of horror into teachers and parents alike but it is to be encouraged as, from such change, comes growth and evolution.

Somewhat appropriately, if we think of the Death card of the Major Arcana, when it is drawn for James Bond by a seductive Tarot reader, the script writer is trying to tell the audience that James might die. This is of course ridiculous on two levels. Firstly with a seemingly unlimited number of rugged actors, and his ability to dodge a barrage of machine gun bullets, we all know James Bond is immortal. Secondly, the Death card does not mean that at all. It symbolises death of the old so that it can be healthily replaced by the new. A reversed Death card, if anything, implies 'real' death and correlates to the way cancer presents itself as the wrong cells 'not dying' when they should.

The Major and Minor Arcana of the Tarot are rich and deep in such symbology and, like our language, the meaning and symbolism of the cards are dynamic. As each new deck of cards is designed, the nuance can shift and indeed new wisdom gets associated with it. Blind alleys can be followed too where meanings that don't work so well get attributed to cards. All change is ultimately healthy though.

Each card therefore contains the energies of all instances of that card from all decks. The same is true of spreads of cards like the Celtic Cross and the triplets I used to form the Recipes of Fresh Thinking. As the intelligence in the Tarot works outside space and time, this includes cards, decks and spreads from the past, present and future.

The same is true of spreads of cards, suits and the triplets I used to form the Recipes of Fresh Thinking.

In this treatise, and with Flavours of Thought, my aim is to deconstruct the Tarot to uncover its root sources and meaning. Whilst doing this though, I am also adding to the collective thought pool associated with the Arcana. You cannot dabble and interact with it without some of it rubbing off on you and some of you ending up in the cards. This is true whether you are just using the deck, writing about it or devising a new deck. So I am making it simpler whilst also adding to its complexity and richness at the same time.

This is just another example of the paradox of our duality. What we do in the Physical Plane affects the 'higher' planes. Activity in the 'higher planes' stirs up action and re-action for us.

The reason incidentally why the Tarot is a pictorial glyph is so it works across languages by using universal symbolic metaphors. This is of course incredibly valuable in the Physical Plane. It allowed the adepts who formed the original decks to collaborate even though they didn't speak each others' language. Some also think that by 'hiding' the meaning of arcane wisdom and suggesting it is a mere parlour trick for fortune telling, they prevented this knowledge being suppressed or even destroyed by powerful 'dark' forces of both politics and religions.

Personally I like this conspiracy story but think there is another version of events that will become clear over the next few years and thtat perhaps I will investigate in a later tome.

The real power in the symbology in the Tarot is that it actually gives a mechanism whereby we can communicate between the Planes of Being.

Remember the Flatland analogy of how we used our fingers to communicate without sound. The 'higher' planes 'speak' to us all the time - and we can communicate with them too. We just have to learn their language.

Each plane too has a preferred method of communication and, once we understand what it is, we realise this communication has been going on all our lives.

It's just been largely one way traffic, from the 'higher' planes down to us. We simply might not have been paying enough attention.

The Archetypal Plane communicates to us by way of 'light bulb moments'. As it operates outside Space and Time, when we get a message from it, it arrives in less than a second. We get the whole image and vision and then it takes seconds, minutes, days and even years or linear time for us to fully decipher its significance.

For example, my first ever introduction to the Tarot was when, in a group workshop, where we all picked a card at random and we were asked in turn to say what we imagined our card meant. Up to this time, I thought the Tarot was to be avoided at all costs and the work of charlatans. When I was handed the Tower, at first it meant nothing to me. When it came to my turn to give my interpretation from 'no-where', I spouted out what turned out to be a pretty exhaustive and comprehensive description of what is generally agreed it meant.

My teacher asked if had I seen the Tarot before and it was genuinely the first time I had knowingly handled a card. This was the Archetypal Plane in action.

This incident piqued my curiosity and started my research which has lead to these books and the healing and transformative work I now find myself undertaking.

The Creative Plane communicates to us in patterns. We see connections and how disparate elements link. From the connections, we forge new constructs. If we have one trait as humans that separates us from the animal kingdom, it's our ability to work out how everything joins up and from there to make new associations. Note though that many primates, some birds and even fish and insects also use tools and have the capacity to reason. We're just particularly good at it. So much so that right now, the cutting edge of scientific research is all focussed on the Big Reverse

Engineering Questions like, "How did we get here?".

The Formative Plane take the seed ideas and the patterns of the ideas and helps us come up with a 'cunning plan'. It helps us see across time how to manifest ideas into action.

Each plane too uses the same mechanisms to 'talk' to us. They are numbers, colours, sounds and thoughts. Light being the carrier and time being the movie allowing them to unfold in a sequence that makes some sense.

The significance of the numbers is told each suit of the Minor Arcana via the cards Ace through to ten. Colours and sounds are vibrations that interact with our ears and eyes. The Tarot is awash with colour and vibration. I recommend you read The Key to the Wisdom of Ages by Paul Foster Case to learn more.

As mentioned before, there is a whole spectrum of electromagnetic radiation that we aren't tuned to like X-rays and radio waves. It's only a combination of our biology and biosphere that dictates what frequencies we are attuned to. If we could pick up other waves, they too would be awash with information.

Some of these waves do sneak through though and are the mechanisms by which some external thought forms are detected.

As for any 'language' that has accumulated over time, the planes combine numbers, colours, sounds and thoughts into 'sentences'. The patterns and numbers are significant. Our lives can be seen as a book with chapters that tells a story with input and direction from the planes.

So you might have the same thought three times. We might associate the image of a red bus with a childhood memory that triggers another thought. This too is significant.

Just imagine the phrase from It's A Wonderful Life with Jimmy Stewart, "Every time a bell rings, an angel gets its wings."

If this phrase pops into your head 'at random' in the future, it's entirely possible that metaphorical 'angel wings' are being conferred on some entity at that time, somewhere out in the Universe.

Nothing we see is actually what we think of as real.

All is sign.

All is number.

All is pattern.

Our role is to decipher and manifest the result in the Physical Plane.

XI : Leaving Cubeland

The adventurous Flatlander who has seen the fingers of a three dimensional creature appear and disappear might wake up one morning with a light bulb moment.

They might start to wonder how they could leave Flatland and explore what must only be a much more exciting Cubeland. After all, when you live in a world with no Up, you can only go 'This Way' or 'That Way'.

There are a couple of ways they could go about this task. Either they could work out how to 'levitate' out of their plane by trial and error. Alternatively, they could request the collusion and assistance from the Cubelander to let them know of their intention.

Flatlanders also dream and meditate so have already had glimpses of this magical Cubeland existence. They have seen tall buildings, flying machines and even magical pyramidal shapes.

Once they learn how to make this transition, they could return to Flatland and teach others how to make the migration too. When enough Flatlanders learn the trick though, something really magical happens. The Flatlanders realise that their world with no Up was entirely of their making and a construct of their collective mind. When enough of them make the transition, Flatland gets its Up!

So when you hear Cubelanders talking about an Ascension, what they really mean is a bidirectional process that involves Descension too. For the next phase of human evolution, the Planes are starting to move and merge. This of course means it's not just about Us. This has implications for all life forms, the planet, the Solar System and beyond. We are talking about a shift in the fabric of Cubeland's Space Time.

The interaction with the Planes is nothing new. It has been an ongoing process since the Dawn of Time which sprang forth, simultaneously with the Physical Plane, from the Formative Plane.

In the past, humankind has attributed mystical and religious connotations to the Planes. So the Archetypal Plane has been referred to as the Creator. The Creative Plane is where the Angels hang out. Our Higher Self, which can see our whole life plan across time, lives in the Formative Plane. From time to time, a human reaches enlightenment and becomes an Ascended Master in the Formative Plane too.

For many people in our secular world, these labels are enough to make them run a mile. I know because I am one of them.

A much healthier and possibly realistic model that I hope will sit well with materialistic scientists is this. The intelligence in each plane is not a separate agency working us as if we are puppets in some illusory matrix. It's more like each form of intelligence is an active agency within each of us and we are manipulating the energies from the planes.

What's perhaps even more significant is that the Physical Plane is not some lowly place where those that have 'sinned' are sent for absolution and to learn. Anyone or anything that can incarnate and survive in the physical realm is an advanced being who knows the tricks of how to pull off how to 'live'. This means even more than ever we should respect every living person, life form and consciousness – good old Mother Earth being foremost in our mind here.

What this means is the Planes are Us and we are the Planes. The same being true for all life forms and matter. I will leave it to smarter people than me to work out the maths. In the quest for a unified theory, they should note that all the clues are in plain-sight in any Tarot deck. For the more insightful explorers, they will also find a simple cube has many hidden aspects and pathways too.

So the Archetypal Plane and the ability to experience and initiate seed ideas is within us and generated by us.

The 'Creative' agency is an integral part of our make up. Our ability to 'Form' plans for the future and memorise the past is second nature. Our ability to dream, think, breathe, eat, sleep and reproduce copies of ourselves is the end result of the mix.

Our ability to be balanced in our gravitation field yet to possess the ability to overcome it - by jumping, flying an aeroplane or igniting a rocket - gives us a clue that not all is as fixed as might seem.

The clues of how to interact with the planes and transcend our cubic existence lie in the corners. Go back to Flatland and imagine a square. If you wanted to teach a Flatlander about Up and how their square can form a cube, you would take them to the corners and get them to imagine an Up.

For Cubelanders to make a similar transition to the Higher Planes, you could suspend them in the centre of a cubic room and point to the corners. You would point them to eight exit points outwards – four on the floor in each corner and four in the ceiling.

There is a choice here however for the Cubelander. The Physical Plane is actually a pretty neat bit of cosmic engineering that has taken ages and aeons to fabricate.

So rather than 'ascending' to some sort of heaven in the higher planes, what might be a smarter and all together cooler idea is to get 'heaven' to come down to Earth to have a 'play'.

The keys to open this door lie in another glyph I came across some years ago called the Cube of Space. I found that the 22 Major Arcana of the Tarot can be placed around a cube. Every cube has six sides, twelve edges, three hidden pathways connecting the six faces and a centre – totalling 22.

When I took the Flavours of Thought and mapped them to the Cube of Space, it became clear I had developed a tool for personal evolution and growth – I called it the Cube of Karma.

About a year ago from the time when I am writing this, I had a rare bout of illness from food poisoning. Note that there are no coincidences and all dis-ease is self generated.

For three nights in a row, I had the same dream in a semi-delirious state. I was taken into a large cube and shown 56 other hidden pathways that are plain-sight on each face. It is no coincidence there are 56 cards in the Minor Arcana.

I since noticed each face of a three dimensional cube can spawn its own cube too. This structure is a four dimensional cube known as a tesseract. A tesseract gives us an idea of what it would be like to add another dimension to our world - note it starts in the corners of the cube.

At this point, this book will now take a slightly different direction. You may have noticed the book's strap line "Towards a Merged Mind" and maybe wondered what that has to do with the book's title and the deconstruction of the Minor Arcana.

Up to now, I've espoused some theories and hopefully provided some illumination. At the very least, I hope I have got the reader thinking differently – even if they are harbouring doubt and incredulity.

The following chapters I hope will bring this all into context. I will show how we can utilise interaction with the planes in our daily lives in order to discover a new way of being.

We are on the cusp of a new Us. This is not some new age 'woo-woo-la-la' movement. This is as 'real' as the 'reality' we call 'reality'. The evidence is all around for those who have been paying attention. For those who haven't woken up yet, the transition is tantalisingly within their grasp.

The keys are in the corners of the cubes of our lives. It pays good dividends to observe what is happening in the corners of our gaze.

Pretty much all this information has been within my grasp for several years. It is only now that I am 'seeing' it and I know from experience that the actual writing of this book is how the story is being unfolded to me.

The chapter sequence now has completely left my original planned mind map for the book. I had also planned to write a chapter a week on each Friday morning. This week has seen four chapters emerging. They are coming in via dreams, reprogramming at night and arriving fully formed during the hypnompic cusp. I am throwing my plans for the day out and writing them instead of all the things I think I 'should' do!

I feel like I am being encouraged to explore how we can all leave Cubeland.

Part 11 : The Return to the Adytum

XII : The Nascent Mind

The last millennia has seen an incredible rise in humankind's understanding and control of the Physical Plane.

One thousand years ago, we didn't really know what the 'Wandering Stars' we now call planets really were. We've now sent probes to most of them and even landed on a few. We've not only split the atom but made new atoms that don't readily exist or form in nature.

We think nothing now of turning on a light switch or speaking to, and even seeing, someone on the other side of the world who we have perhaps never even met in person. Yet, if our electricity supply failed for more than a month, we would be thinking the world was coming to an end. Yet there was no electricity supply even 150 years ago.

It is thought the world is around 4.5 billion years old and probably has about the same amount of time left as it has been around for, until a dying and expanding Sun consumes it. So we have not had electricity on tap for quite a considerable time longer than we have had it. We have experienced at least two mass extinctions in relatively recent geological history. The movement of the tectonic plates has probably erased the evidence of even more.

So if we did experience a disaster of global proportions, the world would not end when the lights went out. Of course, the absence of electricity, and then no Internet connectivity, merely means the life style of some living creatures on Planet Earth has to change. Somewhat ironically it might mean some geeks have to 'get a life'. Perhaps more than any other creature in Earth history, we have done more to change our way of life. Therefore, if a natural disaster altered it, we potentially have the most to lose.

If you could weigh the biomass of the planet, that is the weight of all life forms from single celled protozoa to us, it would come to around 2000 billion tonnes. It would form a sphere with about the diameter of a medium sized town.

Of that, humankind would weigh in at around 100 million tonnes which would be a sphere of around the diameter of the town's central square.

This is not demean our presence but to put things in perspective for what is about to unfold. Perhaps uniquely, we represent the self-aware aspect of that whole biomass. We should though at least include dolphins and whales in the self-aware camp. Perhaps they are performing a role in the aquatic world which is similar to our own.

The other 'unique'ish' quality we possess is the illusion of the disconnection from the Planes of Being and sense of group consciousness. This connection is present in most animals and even operates inter-species in the form of symbioses. The simplest way for us to foster this nascent ability is to get a pet. As dog and horse whisperers demonstrate, higher and deeper levels of communication are possible still.

What our uniqueness brings to the party is this. It only needs a small percentage of the biomass to possess a new level of connected self-awareness for the whole planet to evolve to a new level of being. We are getting close to this point.

Most of the 100 million tonnes of biomass we call humanity are of course completely oblivious of any of this. Again, this is not be frowned upon or looked at from any elitist position. In retrospect, it will become clear why this was all part of the plan. You can't readily find something and value it unless you lose it first.

Like the Flatlander that doesn't even have an Up, most people don't look up much past the top of the tallest building, tree or mountain they might be right next to.

If we have such lack of perception about of three dimensional world, how can we possibly entertain, envisage and manipulate anything much more complex?

This has been one of the main reasons we have been kept behind the Veil for so long. When we pull it back, however, a veritable Adytum awaits for us to explore.

Now when we talk about pulling back the veil and reaching heightened states of consciousness, it's important not to let any elitism to sneak in.

For example, some people partake in championships demonstrating astonishing feats of memory recall. As amazing as it is to recall the value of Pi to 67,890 decimal places, the feat in itself is no more amazing than a bushman's ability to hunt.

The most amazing facility of mind is simply that any human being has incarnated and gained self awareness. For stardust to pull off the trick of becoming sentient is simply miraculous and something we take for granted - until we suffer from mental impairment.

So being able to speak nine languages, play concert grade piano or juggle seven objects at the same time is just a bonus. Given the right conditions and level of motivation, most of the 7 billion or more people on the planet can be taught any of these skills and more. Naturally some of us have a predisposition to some skills over others. Our skills have both an inherited and learned component.

At my height, the long or high jump would not perhaps be sports that give me the best chance of an Olympic medal. I am sure though, if I put my mind and body to it, even at over 50 years old, I could surprise myself and others how far and high I could jump. If I was ever in danger where these skills were needed in a hurry, an adrenalin rush would augment my jumping ability.

Despite our incredible mastery in science, arts, sports and humanities, the vast majority of people on our planet have a mind which is largely nascent. By disconnecting from the higher planes and enjoying a completely materialistic existence, we are missing out on a whole other level of being.

Each one of us is capable of increasing our super-sensible powers. A nascent mind is not a dormant or sleeping mind, it is merely a mind which is capable of becoming 'fully alive'. We all possess nascent skills that have been misunderstood, ridiculed or even the subject of persecution and demonisation.

Each one of us possesses the ability to heal ourselves and others. While we have made incredible advances in medical science, many ailments can be better treated using traditional healing techniques.

Naturally some regulation, trading and ethical standards are useful and some people are more predisposed than others to dispense healing. As an electronic engineer who was oblivious to, and sceptical of, any of this for over 40 years, I can testify anybody's healing powers can be activated. A doctor's surgery is one of the last places I would think to go on the rare occasions I am unwell.

We also possess the ability to 'see' the future, pick up external thought forms and even bend time and space. Precognition and telepathy are natural conditions easily taught and demonstrated. It might also sound fantastical but levitation and bilocation are also skills we possess. The fact that we don't see people floating around and disappearing and re-appearing is just that we would be a danger to ourselves and others if we could do it. There is inherent self-preservation is built into the 'system of planes' to prevent them from tearing apart.

Unless you think this book has taken a bit of a strange turn, I can testify that I have either personally experienced all of these feats except bilocation (as far as I know). I have met many modest and mild people, with no axe to grind, who have bilocated - many in childhood.

I also know that it is vital that these powers are used ethically and not for personal gain. So called 'black magic' bounces back on its source.

Learning to use these skills is easier than is thought and, in some ways, the rest of this book is a gentle introduction to what have previously dubbed 'The Dark Arts'.

You will actually see that tapping into the energy and intelligence of the planes are actually 'Light Arts'. Light itself being one of the conduits of interaction between the planes. Indeed, we are Beings of Light and light crystallises via our aura to form our physical form. Seeing and perceiving the aura by the way is a natural by-product of interacting with the planes.

If you wrote about televisions and mobile phones in a book even 100 years ago, you would have be branded a dreamer at best and a crackpot at worst.

We are on the cusp of a revolution of even greater magnitude as we explore the real powers of our mind during this century. I am sure too that mind-technology interfaces will appear and be perfected. Our descendants will be using devices that seem to us as outlandish and fantastical as an iPhone would to a Victorian.

The changes that are afoot however will threaten and challenge many. The pharmaceutical industry will have to change as people self-heal and heal each other. We will question the use of insurance policies when we learn we only have to 'ensure' our thoughts don't manifest anything we have to 'insure' against.

At a more basic level, we can all learn new techniques that are really helpful in our daily lives. For example, I teach authors how to tune into 'future memories' so they can 'see' the words they have yet to write. This skill can be used in any field of creative or inventive endeavour. Noting that there is a built in karmic safe guard that prevents us from seeing the Lottery Results.

This will lead to a whole new set of job titles in business. Noting that about 40% of job descriptions we have today did not exist even 10 years ago. Personnel Directors will become Chief Wellness Officers. Chief Inspiration Officers will literally breathe life into business ideas. The smarter businesses will employ sages and seers as non-executive directors so they can utilise their ability to interact with, and influence, the future.

More importantly, intelligent interaction with the planes in the creative, production and even marketing cycles will become common. If we are really lucky, we might even drop the 'man-made' false calendar and return to natural 13 Moon time.

We are much better conduits of thought than generators of thought. Tuning Out is the new Tuning In. Learning to allow our thoughts to flow, as opposed to pushing our thoughts and will on to the world, leads us to a whole new way of being.

It is also the key to accessing the planes and to bringing their magic into the Physical Plane.

XIII : The Flow of Thought

As for our breathing and the beating of our heart, we don't give a second thought to our thought stream, and its flow.

Pretty much from the moment we awake until we fall back into sleep, our thoughts follow on from one another. Of course, they are modulated and altered by events that go on around us. They follow patterns, get tied in knots and loops and go off at tangents.

Only in meditation, when day dreaming or perhaps when walking in nature, do we let our minds go quiet and reset.

What we are completely oblivious about when we are behind the 'Veil of Illusion' is that our thoughts are not merely generated in our brains. A closer analogy is that our three dimensional form is riding like a surfer along a multi-dimensional cascade of thought. Sometimes the cascade is like a gentle stream.

Other times it is like a torrent. It has eddies, currents, whirlpools and 'waterfalls' - perhaps better described as 'mind-falls'.

For some, their mind can be trapped in a bottomless pit of depression. Others might be on top of a high mountain with a clear 360 degree view all around. These lucky explorers will have their path going forward well illuminated. They may have followers catching them up from behind.

We are so bombarded by external influences, some days we don't know if we are coming or going. So to get an idea of how the flow of thought operates, and how you can control it, just imagine how a sole occupant of a desert island might be thinking on a day to day basis.

Our desert islander, by the way, happens to be a stranded ex-military helicopter pilot who crashed there some time ago. As he stole the helicopter and disabled all its transponders and its radio, nobody ever came looking for him.

His sole focus was now how to be rescued and get off the island.

The island has abundant food sources, a perfect climate and our occupant has no predators, snakes or biting insects out to get him. He has no real worries or concerns and nothing to do all day. He has no agenda, no distractions, no TV to watch, no books to read, no Internet connection and no phones ringing.

With nobody to talk to he can only 'chat' with himself and his surroundings. All he can do is think and talk to himself.

For some people of course, I may be describing heaven and for others, hell.

Every morning, his routine was to walk around the island clockwise, looking out to sea for passing ships. On each of the beaches he had methodically built a fire over time which he could light at a moment's notice should he see a ship. None had come past.

When he returned to his starting point he made a mark on a rock of how many days he had been on the island. The current count was 312.

The next morning, the 313th, he awoke from a vivid dream about clocks going backwards and he had the radical notion to make his morning trip around the island in an anticlockwise direction. He started noticing features he had never seen before.

He'd never noticed before he'd built 12 fires on 12 beaches. Every third beach had a rocky outcrop extending into the sea. It then dawned on him that his whole island was like a clock face.

The next day, he decided to walk across the middle of the island instead of circumnavigating it. Knowing his stride was about a metre long, he had the bright idea to measure the diameter of his island.

When he got to the other side he had taken 1000 strides exactly.

He was so obsessed with counting he hardly paid attention to a round structure 500 paces in. When he got to the other side of the island, he then walked around half and made the 314th mark on his rock.

Then another light bulb moment came in. From school, he remembered the value of Pi being 3.14 or something. With a diameter of 1 kilometre, he realises his island must be exactly 3.14 kilometres in circumference. Why had it taken him exactly 314 days to work this out? He felt there had to be an external hand at work or, at the very least, some amazing serendipity.

On the 315th day, he decided not to waste any more time looking out to sea for salvation but to explore the interior of the island some more. When he returned to the centre, he climbed on top of the circular structure he'd overlooked while busy counting his steps. He'd chosen a particularly clear day and in the distance, his trained military eye was drawn to clouds on the horizon. There was no mistaking what he saw. Beneath the clouds he spotted unmistakably a land mass he'd never seen before from sea level.

He'd found the place he needed to light his fire. He would be back here that very night fall.

Now this is obviously a made up story. It describes though the flow of thought from the Archetypal Plane of seed ideas through to physical action. Somewhere in the middle, we notice the patterns of what is all around us and form a plan, or follow a process, to lead us to a conclusion in the material world.

When our minds are absorbed in self talk, we block these initial seed ideas coming in and thus anything else that might follow. When we are swamped and influenced by external thought forms from other souls entrapped in the same illusion as ourselves, we miss the significance of how everything fits together.

It's estimated we have around 50,000 thoughts a day although it's not clear what those who are counting call a thought. For example, many people ruminate on conversations past or future or are enwrapped in internal self-talk. What ever the number is, if you spend all of them in fear, concern or worry, inspiration and ideas won't get a look in. If you spend the day with your head in the clouds, nothing will get done either.

This very book, and where it leads me next, is 'real world' example of the flow of thought. This book came about from a seed idea I had when writing my book on light bulb moments - perhaps somewhat appropriately.

While writing that book, I had the idea that thoughts, like light, come in different colours, or flavours. It then dawned on me that the Major Arcana of the Tarot brilliantly described each of these flavours and how they interact with each other. I then distilled the essence of each card into an attribute I called a "Flavour of Thought".

I had some knowledge of how the Tarot maps across the Planes of Being. So I then made some recipes using triplets of cards with one selected from each plane. Each recipe starts in the Archetypal Plane, then crosses the Creative and the Formative Planes before ending up in the Physical Plane at The Obvious - or the Fool.

As the recipes follow this natural order, they operate at a deep level in our psyche and therefore work intrinsically. They are in essence modern day spells.

So unconsciously I had followed a logical sequence and this allowed the book to be written quickly and not require much of an edit apart from a few typos. The way the flavours are laid out is the pattern as defined by the Creative Plane. The recipes follow a process from the Formative Plane. The conclusion ends up in action in the Physical Plane.

For well over two years, I also knew the Tarot mapped on to the glyph known as the Cube of

Space. I even had a flat cube I had never assembled sitting on my desk for ages.

After a while, I cut it out and formed it into a three dimensional cube, yet still did nothing with it. Then one day it dawned on me that the Flavours of Thought would map on to it and, from nowhere, the Cube of Karma appeared. Since then I've realised I'd inadvertently stumbled across a tool of significant personal transformation.

This tool has now been morphed by others into other Cubes to help with children, change, creativity and even relationships. I also now know there are 56 hidden pathways on the Cube to which the Minor Arcana can be mapped. This will be the seed for a further exploration.

I'd also had two books in my library for years on the Tree of Life which I found inaccessible and difficult to understand. Replacing the Tarot references on the Tree of Life with the Flavours of Thought suddenly brought everything into crystal clear focus. Another tool for personal transformation appeared, as if by magic and as easy as pie. It's even called the Tree of Thought, somewhat appropriately.

If you were that stranded helicopter pilot living on an island that has a clock face mapped on to it with a circumference of Pi, it is difficult not to think external intelligence is at work in our cube-shaped world. Like that pilot, I had everything laid out in front of me but could not see the wood for the trees.

If your are of secular persuasion, be comforted by the notion that such an 'external' intelligence may merely be an unexplored aspect of ourselves. We just can't see it from our position at 'sea level'. You may feel that the notions of higher selves, ascended masters, angels, archangels and a Creator better explains everything. Both notions, and all shades in between, may be right. What is of more importance and relevance is how we manifest ideas that percolate down from the higher planes.

It is worth considering that the ancients 'knew' a thing or two thought that we often overlook. Their descriptions of how everything work might sound simplistic and even naive nowadays. By understanding the underlying and overarching metaphor however, considerable insight can be gleaned.

The planes map into the four elements of Fire, Water, Air, and Earth which are represented by Wands, Cups, Swords and Pentacles of the Minor Arcana.

In the schools of Ageless Wisdom, the element of fire represents universal radiant energy from the Archetypal Plane and is represented by the letter "I" in Hebrew.

The element of water represents the fluidity of the cosmic 'mind stuff' of the Creative Plane and has the letter "H" associated with it.

We use our breath to stir up the element of air from Formative Plane. The letter "V" is associated with it.

The Physical Plane naturally has the element earth associated with it. It too has the letter "H" associated with it.

Together the planes spell IHVH which is pronounced "Jehovah". This is the proper name of the God of Israel in the Hebrew Bible, which you will also hear as "Yahweh".

The ancients clearly 'knew' a thing or two. Sadly, some of this knowledge morphed into dogma and false worship as opposed to understanding. By deconstructing and looking beneath the interpretation, we can get to see the real meaning and significance of what is going on.

Our world is a world manufactured from thought. When we learn how to interact with the planes and to 'think' them into action, we can cook up no end of gastronomy.

XIV : Plane Interaction

Every second of every day and even while sleeping, we are in constant interaction and dialogue with the Planes of Being.

A certain level of magic comes to us though when we interact with the planes with conscious volition. It is only then that we realise what nascent power is within our grasp. Of course, it pays dividends to use this power wisely and ethically and not solely for personal aggrandisement.

In order to tap directly into the Archetypal Plane, our conscious mind must go quiet. We have to enter the meditative state. The best technique to use here is vipassanic meditation where we focus on our thoughts such that they collapse in on themselves.

With a little practice, you can even enter a deep vipassanic state with your eyes open. When you do this your brain emits delta and theta brain waves. Note these are a byproduct of the state not the generator of the state.

Nowadays, you can even get meditation machines with headphones and glasses that help induce these states with eyes either open or closed.

As a purist, I feel it better to learn how to achieve this state naturally. Being blessed with dogs that willingly go for a walk at a drop of a hat is a great way to healthily forge and strengthen that connection.

The hypnopompic point on the cusp of sleeping and waking is also a time when we naturally are connected directly to the Archetypal Plane. This is because it is our awakened consciousness that activates the time-based Formative Plane into action, thus invoking access to the Creative Plane.

If you are a therapist, healer or coach, it is really useful to learn how to tap into the Archetypal Plane on demand. It means you can be having a conversation and dialogue with your client while simultaneously receiving insights and wisdom to help with the session.

If you are a writer, artist or musician, we call this connection our "Muse". So for example, before I wrote the last chapter (and indeed all these chapters), I meditated first. Prior to entering the meditative state, my conscious mind asks for information. For the last chapter, I requested a useful metaphor to help illustrate the concept of how our thought streams take us over during each day.

The idea to explore the thought stream for the sole occupant of a desert island, with no external influences except the notion to be rescued, came in fully formed. Only after I wrote it did I realise the multi-level power of this metaphor. We are all like that stranded pilot looking to get off our island, to get back to our old life or to start a fresh one.

Next I had to invoke the Creative Plane. Here's where I had to tell a story of the islander's path to enlightenment. I used a mind map to plan out a few days activities for our hapless pilot. The free association quality of the map lead me down unexpected paths, such as invoking the value of Pi and the metaphor of the clock face on the island. None of this was planned except using this consistent methodology I use to write and create.

An artist incidentally might sketch and a musician may jam until the form of their work takes shape. At this point in their 'musing', they are connected with the Creative Plane.

From such ambulations comes the shape of the piece. The story of the desert islander is of course a metaphor for my own wanderings as I stumble over these esoteric gems in my attempt to understand and explain them to myself and others.

Much of my personal mission to make the esoteric and hidden into the exoteric and known is largely undertaken without knowledge of where this is all leading.

I am having fun exploring and am more like a child in a sweet shop than a wise Oracle in a cave.

So the seed idea takes shape from input from the Creative Plane. The Formative Plane gives it structure. The technical and physical capabilities of the writer, artist or musician grounds it into the Physical Plane.

The hands of the artist paint, although some use feet or even their breasts in the name of art. The fingers of the musician pluck the strings of a guitar or tickle the ivories of a piano. Singers use their vocal chords to modulate the air waves. The writer types or dictates their words. Other technicians might take their outputs and craft them into books, albums and photographs.

Each person in the creative chain will add something to the work by tapping into the planes.

A picture framer can transform a canvas so it is fit to hang in a gallery. A record producer can create a symphony from a few samples. A book designer can make a draft manuscript into a work of art that would be pride of place on any coffee table.

What makes this all effortless is when we go with the flow. If we try and go from idea to output without giving something shape and form, we can end up having to rework and redo work. Due diligence pays dividends.

What's more there are cosmic forces at work here too. Our four seasons directly correlate to the Four Elements and the Planes of Being. The four phases of the moon also have a correspondence as do the times of our days. These mappings though are quite individual and have some relation to the date and time of our birth. They also map to the date and time of the genus of an idea or the date a business was formed, for example.

I have shown the Moon Phase correlations below. A treatment of how the diurnal and annual phases map to each of us is beyond my current understanding and the scope of this book at this time and in this edition. It is worth noting however that even as I write these words, a seed has been sown from the Archetypal Plane that this should be explored. I am comfortable with the notion that a reader of this book runs with this idea and writes the book on this subject.

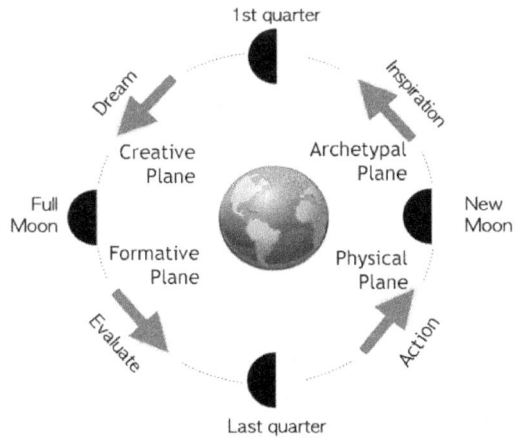

It is worth sharing with you though that I am fully aware of the best times when I am at my creative peaks. This saves me having to push water uphill. All the chapters of this book are written between 8am and 11am, after I awaken and meditate and before I look at emails and take client bookings.

Furthermore, only after I had written and published three books did it dawn on me that I wrote them all in Spring. Note that our language gives us clues of the temporal nature and aspects of the creative process. Things "dawn" on us and this latest book is "springing" into formation. In autumn, I publish and thus plant the seeds for coming seasons and years. In winter, I research and plan the next book or deliver a project or spin off from the previous Spring's output.

As I mentioned before, the times when we are at our creative best is individual to each of us. To work it out, either go back over projects you have completed successfully and analyse their dates. Alternatively going forward, keep a diary and log how creative you feel at different times of the day and the month.

Note that referring to months as 'moonths' gives a clue as to what is really going on in front of our noses. Take some time to notice the Moon phase and even say "Hi" to Sister Moon, acknowledging her for the consciousness that She is

XV : Your Inner Oracle

One of the most obvious practical applications from interacting with the intelligences from the planes is to use them to get answers on absolutely any question.

This can be used for insights into personal matters. In business, you can use it for product or marketing ideas. Scientific researchers, teachers, students, politicians and economists can all benefit from awakening their inner oracle too.

Some people are natural at it and I think businesses would profit by having seers [or see-ers] on board as non-executive directors. Indeed many successful businesses already have such sages at their helms, many of whom may be completely unaware of their innate abilities to see and interact with future memories accessible via the planes.

This principle is, of course, what Tarot readers tap into. There is a big caveat however with all fortune telling services and it is this.

If you 'see' the future for someone other than yourself, you MUST NOT TELL THEM.

This might sound like it will put many people out of business but it is unethical in the extreme to tell others of their fate. What such practitioners have to do is moderate how they impart the wisdom that they pick up such that they steer the client towards their optimum future path. You can only point them gently in the right direction. Merely telling someone they will meet and marry a dark haired stranger and have 2.4 kids robs them of their Free Will. It is like spoiling their 'game' in the Illusion.

To keep this chapter completely ethical, I suggest the principles I will share should be used for personal reasons only. It is worth adhering to generic professional standards for coaching and therapists if you want to use these techniques on others. Asking for permission, for example, is one of the first principles to uphold.

You cannot merely ask an oracle (in this case, you) to tell you the future or give you a gem of wisdom that will be beneficial right now.

There is an art to asking the right question. Ask the wrong question and the oracle's answer will be vague, misleading or unsatisfying. A simple question might be about choice about moving in one or more directions. This can be better phrased by giving multiple specific questions on each of the directions.

For example, I once asked a medium which of two books I should write first. Their answer, by the way, resulted in this book, its prequel and the sequel I am yet to write. I would have got here quicker had I asked two questions like:

"What are the benefits of writing book A?"

"What support and information do I need in order to write book B?"

We should also ask ourselves what is our motivation by asking the question in the first place. If I was really honest, I really wanted to know what was my quickest route to fame and fortune. Now if I had actually directly asked that question, I might have been given an insight about building the consciousness raising portal that arrived 18 months after 'book B' was written.

'Book A' by the way is my novel about the near future of the Earth and humanity which seems to have been put back again by the imminent arrival of the sequel to this book. As it starts in 2087, I still have some time!!

If we ask an open question that starts with 'which' or 'why', it is all to easy for judgement and personal opinion and bias to sneak into the answer.

Questions starting with 'what' and 'how' allow more objectivity and closure.

We should also look for the real question and motivation 'behind' the question. Then when we have identified that new question, ask again what question is behind that.

Repeat this process a few times until you can't think of any other questions and feed the last question you come up with into the oracular process.

So there is as much art and skill into asking the right question as there is in delivering and interpreting and acting on the answer. Like all these things, practice makes perfect and 20:20 hindsight and review of old answers informs and imparts so much inner-sight, often years after the initial 'reading'.

Armed with an appropriate question, there are essentially two ways to go about getting the answers - either without or with a prop. The prop in this context can be a set of cards.

Here's how to 'ask your inner oracle' using the principles from the last chapter on interacting with the planes. This purist method has the benefit of being completely free and it can be done at anywhere and at any time.

The diagram overleaf shows how the answer will percolate down through the Planes into your awareness.

Archetypal Plane

Ideas

Creative Plane

Patterns

Formative Plane

Processes

Physical Plane

Actions

To start with, it is worth writing your question on a bit of paper as this brings it into the Physical Plane. Then prior to meditation, a walk or even going to sleep, stare at the question for 30-60 seconds.

When you do this, look right at the question but defocus your eyes at the centre of your vision and 'look' up, down and left and right of the piece of paper.

Alternatively, if you want to literally 'dream up' the answer, put the paper under your pillow before you retire at night.

During your trance, or dreamlike state, you will get some insight or genus of an idea, even if it's just an inkling or a single word.

Next, then dream up ideas by imagining all the ways this seed idea or word could be used in your life. This taps into the Creative Plane.

Then we begin to form a plan by connecting with the Formative Plane by adding timing and flow to implementation of the dreams and ideas.

Finally we bring it into the Physical Plane by writing down the answer of what comes up. So by way of example, here's 'one I did earlier' which self-references this chapter.

Question:

"How can I best offer my services as an Oracle to people and business?"

As I am reasonably tuned in as I am writing this chapter, the answer came straight back from the Archetypal Plane:

"Your thinking is too linear and ego-centric."

It was then followed by insight from the Creative Plane:

"Just think of all the other ways you can dispense this service with your knowledge - iPhone apps, Mind Map templates, MP3 recordings, workshops."

Further crystallisation came from the Formative Plane:

"Teach others how to become Oracles themselves and do not keep the secrets to yourself."

Simples!

Then the actual answer for the Physical Plane:

"In the past, this knowledge had to be kept secret otherwise it could be used for the wrong purposes."

[This maybe an Atlantis reference as I was told by a medium I was a Child Oracle once - I have no memory of this though.]

"Now the secrets can be shared and taught, don't keep this to yourself, share it by way of a simple eproduct and the businesses will find you if they need you."

So all of a sudden, so many new doors have opened. If I worked flat out, I could only maybe do 8 answers a day, 5 days a week. I would burn out supplying the answers and all the admin and follow up.

By teaching others, who then teach others, there is unlimited scope for this work.

Even though I had planned to write a chapter on this subject, I can honestly say that I didn't plan to ask this question as an integral part of this chapter and I certainly hadn't 'foreseen' where it would lead. I don't even mind if someone else runs with this as I know there is unlimited potential for us to tap into.

As a result of this self-referencing question, I am now contemplating designing an e-course, and possibly a workshop, in practical magic.

Before you learn how to 'read the cards' with this course or anyone else's for that matter, it is worth practising tapping into your Inner Oracle as honing this skill makes you a much better card reader. Note that getting your clients to do the readings and interpretation themselves makes you an even better 'reader' still. It just takes a little trust to let your ego take a back seat and to allow the answers to come from the client.

XVI : Through the Veil

If there is one thing to note from the last chapter, it is this.

We are able to tap into each of the Planes of Being 'at Will' and any time we like. Furthermore, when we tap into information from them in the sequence of the Cascade of Thought, we are able to manifest seed ideas into the Physical Plane with ease.

The Magician from the Major Arcana depicts what is going on pictorially. At his disposal, on a square table to his side is a Wand, a Cup, a Sword and a Coin (symbolising Pentacles). His right hand is pointing the Above and his left hand to the Below. The symbology is that the Four Elements, and Planes of Being, are ours to enlist and manipulate and that we are the connector of the Above to the Below.

So, unlike the Flatlander who is unaware that there may be other dimensions, we can both acknowledge their existence and use them. When we do this, we start to see through the Veil of Illusion and begin to experience a new level of human existence.

Of course, many human beings are happy to be oblivious of this capability and choose to live a 'flat' existence locked in three dimensions and trapped in linear time.

Now there is nothing new, other than perhaps the context, in what I am saying here. Many have trodden this path before and indeed laid the foundations for others to follow. Indeed, the Major and Minor Arcana are awash with clues for the curious of mind and pure of heart. As mentioned, many of the clues are 'hidden' in plain sight.

I should stress again here that it is easy for elitism and ego to sneak in when we begin to develop super-sensibilities. Evolution is intrinsic to our nature and it is important to have people at different stages as each helps the other. By far the best teacher is the pupil of the teacher.

To peer through the veil, we have to remove some masks first. One of them is ego. If it is possible to elevate ourselves from what is considered the 'normal' trapped state of humanity to a heightened state of awareness, it is logical that there are even more states above yet again. I suspect the number of states is close to infinity and climbing back up them is part of the Grand Plan to return to Source.

If we harbour thoughts of ego and betterment through use of new powers, things will backfire on us. Only those with pure motives working with unconditional love will advance rapidly up the steps. When we have thoughts of ego, this activates self-talk. Self-talk keeps us bonded to the physical realm and blocks information cascading down from the higher planes.

Even more insidious than ego and self-talk, is the harbouring deep inside us of any negative emotions. If we are angry, fearful, sad or guilty, these feelings bond us tightly to the earth plane.

Once blocks that have held us back disappear, it is wise to set up future goals based not on targets but on what we want to learn. This unleashes forces and intelligences from the higher planes to work with us to deliver our dreams. Learning based goal setting delivers way above expectations whereas target based systems are intrinsically limited by experience and imagination, and are often based on ego.

With our slate cleansed, we are all set to start interacting with the planes and to peer through the veil. The first technique to invoke is some form of daily meditative practice. If formal meditation is not your thing, a daily walk in nature is often just as effective.

What is also effective is embarking some form of artistic endeavour which engages both brain hemispheres. Combining meditation with artistic practice is even better still.

So get used to taking 'me-time', write that book you have longed to write, go to that art class or learn that musical instrument you have only dreamt of playing.

These are the first steps in tuning in.

Note that meditation and giving yourself 'me time' is the safe way to do this. I have met many people who have had their 'awakening' through trauma and some even from 'Near Death' experiences. I don't advocate this extreme approach unless it happens to be on your karmic path and it's what you specifically want to learn and experience.

Working with glyphs such as the Tarot, the Tree of Life and Cube of Space can also activate new capabilities in us.

There is one big caveat here. Pure left brained knowledge of such glyphs does not always lead to enlightenment. In fact, it can take the student down a path of 'en-darkenment', with their ego and self-talk active in the delusion that the sheer amount of knowledge somehow equates to power.

When you start to tune in, your world begins to take on a new quality. You begin to experience more frequent flashes of inspiration. These are the seed ideas from the Archetypal Plane. Your creativity and productivity increases. You get more done as the Creative Plane channels through you. Plans form much more easily as the Plane of Formation comes under your behest. Lastly, you make things happen in the material world as your Inner Magician becomes a force to be reckoned with.

During this process you will realise the signs have been around you all the time.

Where you encountered resistance, all that was happening was 'someone' or 'something' was nudging you in a different direction. Depending on your belief set, this could be your guides or Higher Self, or quantum entanglement with your perfect future self, pulling you in another direction.

Where you chanced across serendipity, these are signs you are 'on path'. Irrespective of your creed or faith, it's only polite and respectful to give thanks at these times as such acknowledgement seems to generate more strokes of good fortune. Thank Lady Luck at the very least.

Both serendipity and resistance also repeat in patterns to bring things to our awareness. Three bullying bosses or three abusive partners should be enough to tell most people that something is out of kilter.

The Planes also 'speak' to us through signs and numbers. You will see car number plates, observe the clock at times like 11:11 and 5:55. I have lost count of the times that my head hits the pillow precisely with 22:22 or 23:23 on my bedside clock or when I am awoken exactly at 3:33am or 4:44am.

You may also experience step changes in your awareness. When you let fears go, this creates a void in which new intelligences, or 'soul parts', can fill. Sometimes these intelligences arrive while you are sleeping; sometimes they arrive in meditation or come in when out while out walking.

This process can also be induced or initiated by a practitioner such as a shaman or Reiki Master. Indeed, I've even trained a number of people myself, called Tour Guides, who can perform what we call Soul Part Integration.

This incidentally I didn't plan to do and 'nobody' trained me how to do it, I just got several 'downloads' from Above. Next clients who I could help serendipitously turned up even though, at the time, I didn't advertise this service.

Proof that I was not imagining it, or making it up, came from people becoming happier, richer and, in some cases, even instantly clear of dis-eases and conditions they had harboured for years.

What's also great about this way of being is how it is nicely infectious. People around you pick up on your 'good vibes' and start to be lucky themselves. They may want to know your secret. What's even nicer is that people who have held you back in the past start to disappear from your life and people who are more on your 'wavelength' just seem to pitch up like magic.

Like all new skills, we become better at them by practising them. Interaction with the planes though and the ability to see through the Illusion is not something you switch on and off for your day job.

We literally become a new type of person and begin to live a new way of life.

This does not mean poverty, obscurity and asceticism. Rather, this 'way of being' is something which is joy-full and brings great wealth of in areas of both our finances and our health and spiritual well-being. If it doesn't, it may mean some fear or guilt is lingering somewhere.

One of the other side effects of peering through the veil is this. We gain the ability to work across time and space.

This may with healing as well as in being able to send and receive information. Some people are also able to perceive the aura and 'see' past and future versions of people in it.

When this happens to you, as it did spontaneously to me, everything moves up a couple of notches. We realise then that we are living a consensual and very convincing 'dream' we call reality.

Before we explore where this may be leading us from an evolutionary perspective, we will explore the purpose and use of conventional dreams within our 'dream of reality' and how they lead to a whole new level of awakening.

XVII : Lucid Awakening

So just imagine if our three dimensional existence was such that when we awaken into a higher dimensional framework, we could 'see' it was all just a very convincing dream.

While we are asleep, there are two main different types of dreams. Namely there are those where we are an actor or observer and there are some where we are more like a movie director. These latter types of dreams, which we are able to consciously control and direct, are called lucid. They are quite often accompanied with astral travelling and out of body experiences.

Is it possible to lucidly 'dream' while in our 'normal' awakened state? If so, we should be able to steer ourselves out of undesirable situations and into a world quite literally filled with our wildest dreams.

Note, before we run wild and get too excited, that there a few caveats to doing this safely, ethically and successfully that will be explored shortly.

So how do we start to control this lucid dream we call our lives? By the way, it seemed to me to be appropriate that when we do so, we call it something like Lucid Awakening.

In my version of our shared, consensual dream, it is no coincidence that while I was pondering writing this chapter, I noticed on the news only last week that lucid dreaming clubs are becoming quite a fad.

Also on the very morning I wrote the draft of this chapter, this note came into my InBox from Mike Dooley's daily Totally Unique Thoughts.

"There are only two types of dreams, Tom. Those that come true. And those that are coming true. Whoooohoooooo!" The Universe

Just noticing these coincidences is part and parcel of the 'awakening' process. If we go about our lives in the same way, the same outcomes will transpire for us.

Only by changing our pattern and behaviours do we conjure up events that are different.

Of course, we have to pay attention to what is going on and notice changes.

It is no coincidence that I had a dream last night that gave me much insight into these possibilities. It's no coincidence as it was a dream I 'ordered' last night to help me write this chapter.

To put this in context, I also used this dream ordering technique when I wrote a chapter on dreaming in my book The Art and Science of Light Bulb Moments. In it, I documented a vivid dream which I can remember to this day on the power of spin off developments. That chapter explained how to request a dream to give insight into a problem or opportunity and how to analyse it upon awakening.

Our dreams full of illuminations that are normally suppressed or inaccessible to our conscious awareness. If you are one of these people who has trouble remembering your dreams, the way to do it is to wake up slowly. Then make a note either mentally or on paper of just the bullet points of your dream. What you then do is to think about what insights these bullet points might give to something occurring in your waking world.

I am writing this draft on what happens to be a Bank Holiday in the UK.

In last night's dream, I had booked not one but two appointments with two different teams from the same large corporate client at 2pm today. This was a client, Sony, who I haven't worked with for over 15 years. Both teams wanted to contract me to develop an accessory product to complement their own flagship product. This is something I used to do but don't do any more so it was at least feasible.

In the dream, which was very vivid, I got in quite a fluster.

Firstly, I couldn't believe I had booked them both for exactly the same time. Secondly, I had booked them in on a Bank Holiday when we had family coming for lunch. Worst still was I am doing different things nowadays and didn't want to go back to a previous version of 'me'. If I took the contracts on, there was no way either that I could take both product developments on at the same time.

Analysis of this dream gives much insight into my current situation in the 'waking dream'. The 'old me' would take too many things on at the same time and work for others rather than on completing my own projects. By being a busy fool, I could not be accused of slacking.

More insidiously though, my own projects could never fail as they never even got started. My fears of ridicule, failure and success were safely managed.

Now I am 'awake' and 'aware' of the significance of the dream, it is time to act on the message. To do this, we can apply a dream analysis process to our waking lives to give us insights to the messages that are all around us. The 'noise' and 'busyness' of our lives obscure the messages that are all around us. Our dreams allow the core message to come in without conscious filtering.

To do the analysis, we can take a period of time which can be a day, a week, a month, a year or even our whole life to date. Get a sheet of paper and mark out three columns.

Write down in the left hand column, all the times you have felt held back. Next in the middle column, write down some words that describe you while carrying out these type of tasks and activities.

Then in the third column make a note of what you can change in your life such to make sure that situation doesn't arise again.

It's then time to observe from a position of neutrality and objectivity. All we have to do in our waking state to awaken even more and to test whether this hypothesis is true is to do nothing. By not acting out the behaviour that causes the situation to occur, it gives space for new forces to come into operation. This can be tough to do at first but the results come along within days.

For me, when I did this exercise, the message was clear. I jump into projects and make commitments far too quickly. I am also a master at creating and instigating new projects. All of this direction of my energy, means initiatives I have already started never get quite finished. When they end up either failing or not quite reaching their full potential, I jump to the next 'big thing'.

Of course, this scattergun approach has allowed me to gather up quite an eclectic range of skills and experiences.

So for the coming weeks, as a result of this dream, I am not taking any more projects or new initiatives on board until current projects are finished and fully actioned.

This has also lead me to writing the next chapter for this book straight away.

It has also lead me to realise something amazing about the Planes of Being that was previously obscure to me.

Could this be Lucid Awakening in action?

For even for me as the writer, as well as you as the reader, I will only know when the next few chapters emerge and get downloaded from the Planes.

XVIII : Even Greater Openness

The word 'ego' has falsely attracted a negative connotation.

We hear phrases like, "He's got an ego the size of the planet" and, referencing the Moon landing, "The ego has landed."

I've heard also heard some describe EGO as being an acronym meaning, "Edging God Out".

Egomania has attracted itself a bit of a bad press. This is a bit of a shame as ego really just refers to our amazing ability to be self-aware. When extrapolated properly, we should all realise that this ability in each of us is a veritable blessing.

In a community of ants, a shoal of fish or a flock of migrating birds, we can only imagine that each individual is experiencing some kind of collective existence. We on the other hand have our individuality.

Each of us can aspire to greatness.

If you are a citizen of the USA, in theory, each of you could become President. With the preponderance and popularity of TV talent shows, even people with diverse and unusual talents can enjoy their 15 minutes of fame. More practically, with the Internet, each of us can share thoughts, words, images and our voice pretty much instantly with the rest of the planet. If you have something worthwhile to say, or just something amusing to share, you can now instantly connect with an audience.

In a world though where we allow a deeper and stronger connection to the Planes of Being, what role is left for ego? The development of our sense of separateness has taken billions of years of evolution. Are we about to throw it away in a movement to some form of 'Oneness'?

This notion alone is what has driven so many people away from religion and created an increasingly secular society. This 'me first' mentality gives rise to the association of selfishness with ego. Many New Age and spiritual movements talk about "Oneness" too, sometimes without really explaining what it means.

Don't get me wrong, group hugs, meditation and chanting can be brilliant experiences. Something has to shift to ensure they aren't just something done like going to Church on Sunday followed by living a less than pure life the rest of the week.

We are on the cusp though of being able to redefine and celebrate our ego as being a truly wondrous ability. When we allow EGO to stand for "Even Greater Openness", new possibilities arise.

All across the world, autocracies based on the old and tired idea of ego are on their last legs and crumbling. The Internet especially means there is nowhere to hide. Collective movements for change and action can be mobilised in minutes and hours. As fast as the recent riots in the UK flared up, a clean up operation was initiated in hours - not by the council or the government but by ordinary people using social networks. There is of course a danger that one dictator is replaced by another and last Summer's riots could flare up again at a moment's notice.

By acknowledging the existence and operation of the Planes of Being, we can have our cake and eat it. We can and should be separate individuals in our three dimensional space.

We should of course realise that hurting someone or something else only hurts us. The opposite also holds. Helping or loving someone or something else will also bounce back at us in a beneficial way.

The connection of individuals and our individuality in the Physical Plane ripples up the dimensions. Our ability to organise and plan augments the collective capability of the Formative Plane. Creative initiatives on good old planet Earth are stored in the collective consciousness of the Creative Plane. These can then be tapped into by other creatives down the line, thus increasing our capabilities and inventiveness.

Seed thoughts we experience here in the form of light bulb moments encourage even more to come our way from the Archetypal Plane.

The word ego is taken directly from Latin and is translated as "I myself". It was most popularised by Sigmund Freud who would have used the German term "Das Ich", which literally means "the I". This popular concept of ego is a product of being 'Behind the Veil' and in the dreamlike illusion that our three dimensional existence is all that there is to see.

In order to see through the veil, we have to consider a slightly different version of our so called reality. This version questions the very nature of ego but, in doing so, it allows us to awaken into a new state of being and a new level of self awareness. This version of events is one that I have experienced personally working with many clients over the last few years. I was completely oblivious to the possibility of this beforehand and still find it a little incredible.

When we take this on board however, the results we can acheive in personal transformation are amazing.

In just one or two sessions, minds can be cleared of clutter and baggage and even long persistent diseases can be cured.

When we incarnate, for many people what happens is that a multiplicity of intelligences come into the same body. Some come and go during our lifetimes too. Only one of them takes the role on of both observer and 'director' of our lives and sits in our heads. Others operate silently in other mind centres in our body such as our gut and heart. Some intelligences work with us while remaining in the higher planes.

Note that in most people, this is a natural state of affairs and it is more than possible to live a full and happy life without being aware of it. That is all part of the Grand Plan.

For most people though, this only becomes an issue when life becomes difficult or they encounter some resistance. All that is happening is that one part of your personality wants to pull one way while the other sees the world differently.

The mild form of this phenomenon is being in two minds about something or other. More serious conditions are described as bipolar dis-ease or even schizophrenia. Dealing with these conditions clinically will always be a half way house solution. The causes manifest and emanate from a soul level.

By seeing ourselves, and our ego, as being a sum of many components, we allow ourselves to awaken into another level of being.

Fears that held us back were only guidance from our gut. Dislike of a particular situation is only our heart mind telling us that they weren't in love with it. Our 'head mind' and the classic centre for our ego to sit is of course free to both overrule and to regret doing so. Only by making mistakes do we learn.

Now if you are wondering what all of this has to do with the Planes of Being, it is this. Only our conscious mind centre has disconnected temporarily from the Planes as a byproduct of our gaining self-awareness and adopting the illusion of separateness.

Our other mind centres are intrinsically still connected with the Planes.

By allowing our 'ego' to expand to take inputs from all our mind centres, we move to a position of Even Greater Openness.

As you will see, when we open all of our mind centres fully, we facilitate a process that brings the Planes quite literally down to Earth.

XIX : Magical Living

In our left brained, logical world where science has become the new god with mastery over the material plane, magic has taken a bit of a back seat.

Naturally we are captivated by stage magicians who script and perform the most amazing illusions. We also have a growing breed of street magicians who defy logic with mind reading feats and sleights of hand. It has always crossed my mind that some of them might use 'real magic', sometimes referred to as magick, but not be owning up to it. If so, good on them!

Real magic involves the use of mind to create 'real' world change. It is real alchemy and the act of turning 'lead' of thought metaphorically into 'gold', or material activity. In our multidimensional model of the world, this refers to taking an inspiration from the Archetypal Plane via an 8th dimensional thought form all the way down to the Physical Plane.

One of the reasons magic has been suppressed and hidden is that it can be dangerous, or at least unwisely used, in the wrong hands. The word 'occult' means hidden or obscured. The secrets of real magic have been kept from general use to prevent practitioners using it for personal aggrandisement and control.

Once you learn even a few basic magic tricks, if you are bound by the old model of the word ego, you can easily get a bit big for your boots. Even those who use magic for healing can get a little messianic from time to time, wanting to heal the world and sometimes line their pockets in the process.

It is in the interests solely of Even Greater Openness that I believe it is time for magic to come back into fashion. It's said a good magician never reveals their tricks and this should hold true for those wonderful stage magicians.

Real magic can however be used completely altruistically and safely. When we allow it back into our lives, we begin to live a completely charmed existence. Where we previously struggled, we begin to experience the most amazing serendipity. Magical living is also infectious, in a nice way.

Your good fortune rubs off on those you interact with. People around you who previously held you back seem to vapourise. New souls who can help you in your goals up turn up 'at random'.

Real practitioners of magic are all around us. Some are even oblivious to their powers. The most powerful practitioners are meek, humble, charming and sensitive. They often cloak and mask their activities by under professional banners such as a life coach, a dog or horse whisperer or a business angel. Naturally there are some charlatans and some that are just learning their craft.

They are all of course masters at interacting with the Planes of Being. They acknowledge that the power is not within them but channelled through them. As a result they don't take themselves too seriously and are respectful of the forces they are blessed to be able to bring to bear.

Up to now, I have purposely not discussed any detail of the cards in Minor Arcana itself, just the significance of the suits.

Both the Major and Minor Arcana are marvellous tools we can use in our daily lives to allow magic to sneak back in.

So let me share the secret of the most simple of 'real' magic tricks.

My book Flavours of Thought describes the purpose of each card in the Major Arcana as being a modifier of consciousness. As mentioned, when the 'flavours' are combined together in triplets to form 'recipes', what has been concocted is to all intents and purposes is a modern day spell. They work beautifully and sublimely.

Irrespective of which deck you use, the Major and Minor Arcana contain the collective magical intent and wisdom of all deck designers, practitioners and querents both past, present and future. We can use this wisdom in our daily lives without even knowing any detail of any of the cards.

The simplest way to do this, and something I do each day, is to split any deck into Major and Minor Arcanas and shuffle and cut each deck to select one card from each. Then leave them on your desk or bedside table and let their magic work itself into your day.

You can also allow their meaning to influence your day whether you pick up unconsciously what the card suggests to you or you have deeper knowledge of the significance.

I chose the Chariot and the Ace of Pentacles today - or they were chosen for me.

As a result, I am intent to 'drive' things forward to conclusion (the Chariot) and I am being 'single minded' about bringing my current project into the Physical Plane (the Ace of Pentacles). Incidentally the project I was working on in parallel with writing this book was an e-course on how to bend time by changing the speed of consciousness.

If you want insight into a problem or opportunity, there is another simple spread which uses one Major Arcana card (Card 0) and four from the Minor Arcana.

My preferred deck for such readings is the fabulous Creative Brainstorming Deck by Mark McIlroy as it contains all the wisdom of the cards but with no baggage of interpretation. As it has no Tarot branding or explicit references, you can even use it inside businesses, or with people, that would be horrified if they thought you were doing a Tarot reading.

The spread is shown overleaf.

What we take from this spread is a new energy from the central card (Card 0) from the Major Arcana. The four Minor Arcana Cards then give us in turn:

Card 1 : a new sense of direction

Card 2 : a new influence

Card 3 : an indication of where we were heading previously

Card 4 : an indication of how we were influenced previously

For the Major Arcana card, if you don't know the Tarot, use the corresponding Flavour of Thought as your guide. The correspondences are shown in the After Words.

```
                    ┌─────────────┐
                    │   Card 1    │
                    │   Minor     │
                    │   Arcana    │
                    │   New       │
                    │   Direction │
                    └─────────────┘

┌─────────────┐  ┌─────────────┐  ┌─────────────┐
│   Card 4    │  │   Card 0    │  │   Card 2    │
│   Minor     │  │   Major     │  │   Minor     │
│   Arcana    │  │   Arcana    │  │   Arcana    │
│   Old       │  │   New       │  │   New       │
│   Influence │  │   Energy    │  │   Influence │
└─────────────┘  └─────────────┘  └─────────────┘

                    ┌─────────────┐
                    │   Card 3    │
                    │   Minor     │
                    │   Arcana    │
                    │   Old       │
                    │   Direction │
                    └─────────────┘
```

For each of the Minor Arcana cards, pay attention to both the number and the suit. Specifically use the suit to guide you as to whether the influence or direction is operating at the level of the Archetypal, Creative, Formative or Physical Plane.

Now if this all sounds a little simplistic, it is. By way of explanation, here's an analysis of a spread I did today on the Bending Time project using the Rider Waite deck.

Note that I am no Tarot reader and am just giving you the interpretation that 'came to my mind'. This is by far the best way to read the cards in the same way that your own interpretation of your dreams is better than getting one from a book!

Card 0 : The Tower

Card 1 : the Page of Wands

Card 2 : the Ten of Wands

Card 3 : the Four of Swords

Card 4 : the Ten of Pentacles

And the interpretation that came to me just from the imagery of the cards (and no reference to my many books on the subject) was as follows:

Card 0 : The Tower - throw out all preconceptions and limitations, it is time to 'allow' something amazing and huge to come along

Card 1 : the Page of Wands - be resolute in your ideas, they are pure and unadulterated

Card 2 : the Ten of Wands - the load is heavy but your completeness gives you the strength to carry it

Card 3 : the Four of Swords - time to let go of the *laissez faire* attitude as it's a bit like lying down on the job and letting the creative force just wash over you

Card 4 : the Ten of Pentacles - stop being influenced by financial motivations, this will come in easier the 'other way'

Now as I complete the project over the next few days, I will leave that spread on my desk as its magic will weave itself into my world and the Physical Plane.

So just armed with two 'spreads', one with just two cards and one with five cards and pretty much no knowledge of the Tarot, you can bring its magic to bear on your world. Note that one of the reasons the cards of the Major Arcana are also known as Keys is that they unlock hidden talents and potential in us.

Daily use of the cards is the best way to unleash the potential wrapped up inside the Planes and bring its power and wisdom in to what we call the real world. Your investment in starting to live a whole new magical life is just a £10 or $10 pack of cards.

XX : Beings of Karma

When we elect to live a magical life, only two types of events occur in our world.

Either good things happen that can be thought of as confirming we are on our karmic path. Alternatively, we encounter difficulty, hardship or even trauma. These latter events naturally challenge us but they also give us opportunity to learn. We can see them as signs we've slipped off our path, but perhaps for good reason.

Karma is a powerful concept that allows us to gain perspective on both why we are here and what direction we should take in life.

The concept of karma is also one that can easily get hijacked and misused.

Karma is not some kind of cosmic retribution system. It is not a ledger of all the good and bad things you have done. This model for karma is one that only surfaces when people want to exercise a degree of control over others.

Simply put, karma is your collective experience and learnings to date. If you want to think of it as being accrued over multiple lifetimes, that's completely optional.

It is also thought that our karmic path, or mission, can also be preordained and pre-agreed by ourselves. Again it is somewhat academic if this is true or not but just thinking it might be can have real world benefits.

When you flip from thinking that the world might be against you to seeing all events as opportunities for learning and growth, a kinder world presents itself.

The metaphysical stance is that that karma goes with the soul from lifetime to lifetime. One theory I heard was that the parts of soul can incarnate in many bodies both simultaneously and backwards and forwards in space and time. If true, this means any cosmic ledger recording our good or bad deeds would be tricky to maintain.

A materialistic explanation for all of this could be that learning is carried, and passed on, by our DNA and RNA from generation to generation. I am half my mother and father and in turn a quarter of my four grandparents. This could explain how learnings are carried forward in time. It's been noticed that some traits seem to leapfrog odd generations too.

Karma though does not just work linearly forwards with Time's Arrow. A shaman taught me a trick some years ago of how to send messages, or learnings, back in time to earlier versions of you. This further complicates the whole notion of karma as a linear sequence.

Karma describes a path of learning and advancement and that is the context in which it is used here. It is the sum of all our past learnings combined with our intent and actions going forward. If you so choose, this can include past and future incarnations too but this is somewhat academic as there is only one thing you can change and that's what you are thinking and doing right now!

What complicates the issue of karma a little further is the concept of soul parts.

It is part of the illusion of our existence that we are one entity we call ourselves. Each time we incarnate, we come in as an assemblage of soul parts. As we become self-aware, one of them takes the role of being "us" and giving us the magical ability to being self-aware. In the background, the other soul parts operate silently by watching out for us, guarding us and protecting us.

When parts are in conflict with each other, it is this that causes bipolar dis-ease and schizophrenia. Popping a pill does not get to the root cause.

Some of our soul parts of course don't incarnate with us at all and remain discarnate, acting as our guides.

From time to time, as we evolve and grow, new soul parts attach themselves and some older ones detach themselves – this is a continual process operating throughout our lives. All aspects of our being are in agreement with this arrangement. Each component is on its own karmic path whilst also working on the group karma of the collective entity we refer to as ourselves.

Working alongside and along with these familiar aspects of ourselves is a comfortable way to be and sometimes the soul parts stick with us longer than is necessary. This is much like hanging out with old friends from a sense of loyalty rather than a inner-sense that you know you should really move on to new pastures.

While each of the soul parts is working on its own individual karma, collectively the assemblage of 'parts' is working on the karma of the 'group'. This also scales up to families, teams, businesses, countries and even the whole planet. Resolving group karma also works backwards in time by healing the past.

Here's where we can allow connecting with intelligences from the higher Planes of Being to take on a whole other practical role.

In some cases, it is in the interest of all 'parties' for separation of soul parts to occur and for new energies to arrive.

We can see the keys of the Major Arcana and the cards of the Minor Arcana as intelligences. They normally hang around in the higher planes but by working and living magically with the deck, we allow them to manifest and operate through us in the Physical Plane.

The Major Arcana represents seeds that emanate from the Archetypal Plane. The Minor Arcana represent forces from the Creative Plane. When we assemble them into spreads, they begin to take shape in the Formative Plane. We then interpret and manifest the output in the Physical Plane. Note that 78 cards can be configured in trillions of permutations so that a lot of manifestation!

We are not limited of course to the cards in the Tarot. There are many systems that portray levels of intelligence outside our real worldly plane of existence.

Most ancient civilisations would not limit themselves to one god. They enjoyed working with a whole pantheon of deities.

More recently, most world religions like the idea of a single creator, although why they can't agree it must be the same one is somewhat puzzling.

Such a Creator, of course, would sit above all the Planes of Being having created the whole system.

He, or why not She, would then create a whole galaxy of Beings to manage affairs. From our 'lowly' existence, we create hierarchies in an attempt to understand it all.

Archangels perhaps working in the Archetypal Plane manage angels in the Creative Plane. These angels then manage a glut of Ascended Masters in the Formative Plane. These Ascended Masters, and sometimes the angels and even archangels, then act as puppet masters and guides for us humans entrapped in the Physical Plane.

Such a hierarchy, with its reporting structure, is vaguely reminiscent of a business with its CEO, Board of Directors, management team and shop floor. It is of course merely our way of trying to explain the complexities of higher dimensions in terms we can understand. Note that these ideas can be used insidiously by 'high priests' to control others by asking us to defer to 'higher powers' and prostrate ourselves in front of gods of our own making.

More latterly 'Science' has replaced the Creator in many peoples' minds. Blindly following any creed as being the 'gospel' and the one true version of events is both dangerous and sloppy thinking.

For example, a healthier version of what might be occurring can be seen by flipping things completely on their head. Some religions portray humanity as lowly workers cast out of heaven and enslaved in some form of painful experience to redeem our sins. When we go through some form of sacrifice, we will be rewarded with what sounds only like Earthly pleasures in Heaven.

What if though, we were actually the advanced guard of beings who had learned the skill of being able to incarnate into physical matter? This would mean the Physical Plane is Heaven and we are in it.

The point then of the Higher Planes is not for us to ascend into them but for us to act as placeholders and conduits for the Higher Planes to operate and learn in the 'Living' World.

So by working with glyphs like the Tarot, we initiate the descension of discarnate intelligences from the Higher Planes into the Earth plane.

Our sole, or soul, responsibility is to embrace and experience life on this planet. Collectively we can also do this with what ever pantheon of spirits we choose to operate. Note that this can include none for atheists as, if that is your belief, then you are just learning what it's like to live without the concept of there being a Creator. Such differences of opinion should be encouraged, cherished and celebrated, not fought over.

In is such spirit, that the model in this book is explored. It is just a model by which we can explore and attempt to understand the most amazing mystery of being here and being self-aware. I will state firmly that it's not exactly right and that better versions have been proposed before and better ones will certainly come along in the future.

Whatever system or model we adopt though, having a mission to learn as a Being of Karma is an exciting prospect.

By holding an assumption that the cards we have been dealt with can be manipulated and exchanged, a whole new life can open up for each of us.

Collectively this means a whole new physical world can also emerge around us, if we let it.

XXI : Deathless Reincarnation

When we fully come to terms with the notion we are experiencing a three dimensional existence underpinned by a multidimensional framework, a new vista opens up for us.

We accept that one of these additional dimensions just happens to be time, we've called it the fourth, and we merely flow along it. Both past and future versions of us co-exist with the present version of us. We just choose to think our our past as having gone and our future having not yet arrived. I can testify though it is possible to access future memories just as well as those gone by. It is also possible to see past and future 'versions' of us by seeing through the Illusion.

We never really die and we are never really born, these are just milestones somewhere on the experience we call life.

We are in a sense immortal when we live right in each moment.

When we make this leap, it is like our Flatlander accepting there is an Up. More importantly she then decides to live her life as if other dimensions are not a mere possibility but a fact. When this happens, the 'Uplanders' realise they have an open mind and listening ear and begin a dialogue with the Flatlander. It takes the Flatlander a while to fully understand the communication mechanisms of signs, numbers, patterns and metaphors dreams.

For example, I was woken yet again at 3:33am with the content for this chapter. My Twitter followers were at 13333 yesterday, I happened to notice. Someone or something is trying to tell me something.

The benefit to accepting information from the higher planes to the Flatlander, and for us Cubelanders, is that they open themselves to a whole panoply of magical tools. Their compatriots wonder what magic they are weaving. Some may fear them or shun them as charlatans. Others might revere them and put them on a pedestal, if the ego of the Flatlander invites such adulation.

The smart Cubelander just goes about their 'new' business with humility and reverence for the new 'powers' at their disposal. They have full recollection of what it was like to be asleep. They essentially become a 'new person' who has re-birthed without the inconvenience of dying, being born again and forgetting everything.

This is a form of death-less reincarnation and we can do it anytime we like and as often as we like.

Now the purpose here is not to make a case for reincarnation in any shape or form. Whether you believe in it or not is a personal choice. I also suspect that proving it is true or not is near impossible when we are incarnate in Cubeland.

Whether I believe in it or not is somewhat irrelevant. I will state that, even though I seem to be able to 'see' past lives, I don't know if it is true or not. To me, whether it is true or not is more about interpretation than doctrine. On the subject of doctrine, it is believed that reincarnation was even accepted as being part of the Christian faith until the Council of Nicea in 325AD. It is of course more commonly an accepted part of Eastern religions.

Many different models have been proposed for how reincarnation might work from the sublime through to the loosely scientific. Somewhere in the middle are some ideas that are obviously made up for other reasons. For example, I once met a senior figure in a church, both he and that church will be nameless, who was convinced that if you are a man, you can only ever then reincarnate as a man. No advanced soul would ever put that restriction on itself as it would be missing at least half the possible sphere of experience and knowledge.

If reincarnation is at all possible, personally I would love to experience life from the perspective of other animals. I would love to know what it is like to be an elephant, a dolphin or an eagle. Equally, I am fascinated at what life must be like in a collective community as experienced by a termite, a bee or an ant. Life as a Kobe cow, who is fed on beer and massaged for its entire life, also has its attractions.

Other 'schools' put limits on how many times you reincarnate. Others introduce the concept of karma but doled out in some sort of cosmic retribution system so that in one life you might be making amends for previous misdemeanours.

A purer, cleaner and agnostic version of how reincarnation runs something like this. I stress though that this is only a model for us to get our heads around a concept which is unworldly.

There is a component of our being, called a soul, that is immortal. For some of the time, it hangs about in the ether. That said, when you hang about in the ether, time as we know it takes on a different quality, if it exists at all. From 'time to time', the soul decides to incarnate, or it is decided for it. I've heard it said that there is a queue of souls waiting to incarnate on good old planet Earth. Again, any reference like this has to be taken with a pinch of salt, no matter how attractive and how the convincing the teller states it as fact.

Prior to incarnation, the soul meets with a 'soul group' in a place referred to as the Akashic Records Office. It discusses with the soul group what it would like to acheive and experience from its next incarnation and the conditions for birth are set up. The next level of detail is up for debate so don't take it as 'gospel'.

The soul then chooses what it would like to incarnate as - e.g. as a human, fly, horse or some life form not even on Earth - and it also chooses its parents. One version of this process allows for the soul to split into many parts and incarnate simultaneously on either same or different planets at the same time. Note if the planets are separated by many light years, the restriction of the speed of light in the Physical Plane means they are unlikely to bump into each other. That said when you meet someone you think you know from before, one possibility is that they are an aspect of the same soul … or perhaps also the same soul group. Note that another conjecture is that some of your soul group remain in the higher planes and act as your guides while some may incarnate themselves at the same time as you.

As the soul incarnates as a baby and comes down the birth canal, it is programmed to forget what it came to learn in this next incarnation. This, of course, conveniently makes proving all of this slightly difficult. In then learning a new set of tricks in a new context, the soul gets to rise another level during its lifetime. When it comes time to shed the mortal coil, the soul returns to the Akashic Records Office, reviews the life it just had with its soul group and hangs around again in the ether until there's a space on a planet somewhere in the Universe to have another go.

From time to time, having had loads of goes around the loop some souls reach a stage of enlightenment where they 'ascend' and have no need to reincarnate again. They might not even die as we know it but just disappear from the three dimensional illusion we refer to as reality. These souls are referred to as Ascended Masters. Once they have Ascended, they then have more rungs that can be climbed to the angelic realms.

Now I personally like this as an explanation solely because it is attractive and it appeals to my sense of how things should be. If I was to design a system like this, I would make it cyclical in nature and incorporate degrees of advancement and attainment.

It does look remarkably like our academic system in nature though where we go through trials like exams, get reviewed and when we pass, we move on to the next level … and so on. Occasionally, we might have to take re-sits. This could all be coincidental or because it's such a logical system, ingrained in our very being, that we've emulated it in our culture.

If reincarnation is the way things work then, from time to time, it understandable that we would get flashes of recognition, or *déjà vu*.

Indeed, there are many reported and even provable cases around the world where children seem to demonstrate incredibly detailed memories of past lives.

As any system of reincarnation doesn't lend itself easily to scientific analysis, it is probably not worth spending time debating if it is true or not. Certainly, it is not worth defining how many levels there are in the system and how many times you can incarnate. These can only be personal interpretations on something we have little comprehension of or control over. Remembering that, in this model, we also agreed to be programmed to forget all about the finer details.

From the purpose of this chapter though, the idea of reincarnation serves as a metaphor for personal, and even collective, advancement. In this system, we have a go at a life, die and then come back and have another crack at it.

What though if we don't have to wait to die to reinvent ourselves and evolve to a new state of being?

While some people gain enlightenment and sometimes considerable magical powers through undergoing significant trauma, or even a near-death experience.

Just imagine though if we could experience such a shift naturally, safely and painlessly.

The key to such a natural, intra-life rebirthing process is not that our Cubelander rises into the higher Planes of Being. That is too easy and known as an 'old death'.

What our re-birthed Cubelander has to pull off is to bring the Planes of Being into their world.

As a result, they create a new level of Merged Mind.

XXII : The Merged Mind

If you have got this far in the book, you may have spotted that there is a certain irony being played out here.

As mentioned, it's reckoned two or three generations of stars have formed and died over billions of years to form the heavy elements from which we are made. It's taken a lot of cosmic blood, sweat and tears to create sentient stardust that can look and wonder where we came from.

Remember too that it is not just us but every atom of matter in the Universe that is supported by the Planes of Being. The basic concept of a star began as a seed idea in the Archetypal Plane. All star types, from red giants to black holes, were imagined in the Creative Plane.

In the Formative Plane, the process was defined whereby the star formed, shone brightly and then died, either in a spectacular supernova or snuffed out quietly like a candle with no wick or wax.

From a fifth dimensional perspective, the sphere of a star in the Physical Plane looks as flat as a pancake does to us. Indeed, we also look like flat blobs wandering around on the surface of our home planet.

The vast majority of these blobs don't even look up at the night sky in awe. They cannot see past the end of their day and many are struggling to survive financially and to maintain their spirit. The irony is that the amazing magic trick of these blobs being blessed with self awareness has cut them off from the Universe that spawned them, not least the Planes of Being.

In the last century especially, we have mastered the physical domain to such an extent that the very thought of a creative seed intelligence isn't needed. The fact the scientists need fudge factors, like the cosmological constant, to make the equations balance should be clue enough something is missing.

I am not advocating a case for God, if anything I am somewhere between an atheist and pantheist. I run a mile from any dogmatists.

What is clear is despite our amazing ability to space probes out of the solar system and make video phone calls anywhere on the planet, many people are in a kind sleep which is akin to a waking coma.

There are many people who are fully awake, yet asleep to what is really going on around them. For many people, there is an assumption that the cards they have been dealt with are it. Their thoughts mirror those of others and the current collective mood of the nation. If the government and the press say we are in recession, then they believe it.

The world tends to happen around them and they live their lives simply reacting to events around them.

Does this sound terrible? Well no, the fact that a living being can even have thoughts and be self aware is nothing short of amazing. In this state, you can achieve incredible things. You can love, cry, laugh and be in awe of nature or art. You can be entertained and you can entertain others. You can cry, be fearful or guilty, be hurt and be angry.

All in all, this is an amazing feat for something which is around 75% water, 20% carbon and the rest a mix of other atoms. This mind can also walk around largely unaided, feed itself and, in collaboration with others, fly itself to the Moon and back.

Such sleeping minds are not bad minds but they are easy to spot. They might chat incessantly about themselves, their football team or the weather. They might be unlucky in love or in life or fearful of both. They might have one of those egos that are the size of the planet. They might be serial entrepreneurs who have a string of ideas that never quite seem to make it off the drawing board.

When they are not chatting about themselves, they are absorbed by inner dialogue. If you know what you are looking for, you can even see this state of inner chatter mirror on their faces as thought forms race around their neurology.

Fortunately, some 'sleeping minds' might have a sneaking suspicion that there must be more to life than this. Let's call this type of mind "nascent".

The nascent state of mind occurs to those who have been 'asleep' who almost literally wake up one day. If you think about it, you can only wake up if you have been asleep. This awakening realisations can come in the form of a light bulb moment, much like Saint Paul on the road to Damascus or Isaac Newton hit by his apocryphal apple.

Some people are born with a nascent mind but have to grow through some form of 'sleep' as they become self aware and indeed educated in new skills and a new world. These are the bright kids on the block who show extraordinary talent and perspicacity from a young age. From our birth to the development of self-awareness around seven years old, we are undergoing such a re-awakening.

Those who awaken in their 30s and 40s tend to awaken either as their children leave the nest or when they leave the assumed security of the corporate world. Perhaps a redundancy or loss of a family member is the trigger.

Some awakening people become addicted to alternative therapies, visit sweat lodges or try and communicate with other dimensions. If they don't get an immediate result, they can become disenchanted with their experience and end up back in a dormant state.

Some awaken as a result of some trauma or even a near-death and associated out-of-body experience. The near-death experience itself is also another state of mind. People who have had them come back with a different sense of purpose and truer understanding of the nature of 'things'. Some tell of experiencing 'walk in' or a new soul part that joins them for their onward journey.

The route to a nascent mind is much simpler than this. It's to become aware of what is around you and to become awake to serendipity. It's equally important to appreciate both the natural world and 'human-made' achievements and not eschew one over the other. The beauty of a sunset has equal status with the microprocessor that drives your mobile phone. They are formed from the interaction of the same stuff - matter, energy and consciousness. The beauty is literally in the eye of the beholder.

Those with nascent minds are collaborators and team players. They know that 1+1 equals at least 3.

They accept adversity as opportunity and, as a result, they become luckier. They are not limited by the world around them as they have the power to shape it.

They become truly alive and a force not only to be reckoned with but one you want to be around. They begin to live at cause.

One day some people with a nascent mind realise there might be yet another level of awakening still … and ones beyond that.

If you think about it, we can only influence the material world in one of two ways. We can either make a sound and vibrate the airwaves with our body in some form. Or we can touch or hit something.

So we can make sounds that convey wisdom or entertainment with our voice. We can use our fingers, or toes, intelligently to type something, play an instrument, cook a meal or fabricate something. The thing we then create can then itself touch or signal to the world, whether it is an idea or some form of art or even a machine. The machine though is controlled in some way by voice or other fingers (or feet).

So what if we could influence the world in other ways? What if just pure thought could make things happen? What if we could channel energy to heal others across space and time?

Some Cubelanders experience these phenomena spontaneously and start to ask questions about our model of the world.

Other intrepid explorers go out to find answers. Others are perfectly happy to remain asleep. As this is a planet of free will, this latter option is also perfectly OK.

When nascent minds get together, they start to realise there is more afoot. Our conscious, self-aware mind operates at the tip of a large iceberg we call the unconscious mind. What connects our unconscious mind to the collective consciousness is sometimes called the higher self. Some people refer to it as their guide. In this model of the world, all nascent and sleeping minds must be connected together, yet they are capable of experiencing Cubeland separately.

When I was first introduced to the concept of the higher self and guides at a workshop, I experienced something other than the teacher, who was forging the connection, explained would happen. It felt to me as a guiding force came in and merged with my consciousness.

This gave me direct access to the collective. My creativity shot up. I started to know things I didn't know. I began to heal people, sometimes of deep physical and mental trauma, within minutes of meeting them, or even just talking with them over Skype.

I also met loads of people who did the same. I know I am not particularly special and these skills are nascent in all of us.

So I now know there is only a small step to take from a nascent mind into a merged mind. In some ways though, it's also like taking a step back several thousand years to when humankind was one with nature. Everything had a rhyme and a reason and nothing is separate from anything else.

As Chief Seattle was reported to have said, "All things are connected. Man did not weave the web of life; he is merely a strand on it. This we know."

The merged mind is fully open to all possibilities. It treasures every moment and pays attention to every thought. It is as attentive to the external and the internal.

To a merged mind, adversity is seen not just as an opportunity but as a sign. It's a sign that no matter how far they have personally developed; there are still an infinite number of rungs on the evolutionary ladder and still much to learn. The adversity has merely been presented as the next learning.

Those with merged minds are 'mind-full' of the nature of their thoughts and have an amazing capacity to multi-task.

What is happening neurologically is that the merged mind is starting to tap into the 90% or so of the brain that we haven't fully understood yet.

Many children are now being born with merged minds and you may hear references to them as indigo and crystal children. They have amazing capabilities but, as children, they still need to mature and they need much love and support.

From a functional perspective, those with merged minds are attuned to the superconsciousness and are relaxed with the knowledge that most thoughts aren't necessarily their own.

Those with merged minds are creators, catalysts and connectors. They are also meek, humble and thankful of their ability. They are reflective and don't take themselves too seriously.

They seem to possess an unlimited capacity for adaptability, compassion and absorption.

They heal both themselves and others upon a thought.

We are all equipped with the ability to choose which thoughts we have and how to use them to map our way in this world. When our minds merge with all others, we do not lose our sense of separateness, we just think and operate in a whole new way.

What is unfolding here is something quite subtle. The nascent mind is only capable of making a change on the Physical Plane from either movement of the physical body or by making a sound.

Running, shouting, banging, typing, painting, singing, plucking or screaming all use touch or modulation of the air around us.

A merged mind is capable of control of actions and outputs in the Physical Plane by thought and will alone. Healing, manifestation and telepathy are relatively easy skills to hone. Bilocation, levitation and transmutation of matter take some time to master.

The significance of the Tarot in this regard is its use as a magical glyph which instigate the changes in our core to awaken us from slumber into a different state of being. When we then use them in a context of tools such as the Tree of Life and the Cube of Space, even greater and more rapid transformations ensue.

I have 'consciously' avoided making this book into a workbook with exercises. My aim is that is a narrative inspired by the structure of the Minor Arcana only not a description of it. There are some fabulous books available that will describe the Tarot in much more detail than I can, some of which are listed at the back of this book.

This book concludes with some After Words.

These are sign posts and summaries of areas that you can explore on your own. I may well expand on some of them in further works of my own.

If they inspired others to take up the baton instead of me, these books will serve their purpose as other books have done for me.

By working with what looks like magic daily, we can end up living a charmed and happy life.

This book is not a rant and is not a clarion call to follow some new god or for us to do a global group hug. By living each of our lives to the full, together our world will change.

We do not have to go up to the Planes. We can allow them to merge once again with us.

Part III : After Words

The Flatlander who learns how interact with the higher dimensions might look like a bit of a magician to their compatriots.

They could also be seen as a charlatan and, if their ego got too big for them, they might be seen or portray themselves as a high priest.

One of the tricks of a magician's trade is the card trick. Cards, being essentially flat, would work well in Flatland. Our Flatlander magician would draw patterns on her cards that describe allegorically an imagined higher dimensional world. The perfectly drawn cards would even invoke higher dimensional forces.

Well, for thousands of years in our Cubeland, we have had a set of cards that does exactly that. The messages contained in a modern Tarot deck probably date back to Sumero-Bablyonian times. They began life on cylinder seals which, somewhat interestingly, are three dimensional objects.

This is because the Tarot only truly comes to life when we see it in a three dimensional framework.

I suspect its true structure is only apparent from a higher view still.

As the Tarot has such a long heritage, the original messages have been augmented, distorted and even hijacked.

In this section, the aim is to uncover some of the core and original meanings and significance. I should clearly state that this is a personal view only. I encourage you to experiment and form your own interpretations.

By using Tarot, the collective wisdom associated with the whole deck structure, the suits and individual cards increases. The cards become more powerful and useful too. New decks appeal to new sets of people too.

I should start this section with a caveat. When you start working with the cards, what looks like magic starts to come into your life. You will experience a slew of serendipities. People you haven't seen or heard from for years turn up out of the blue. You start to find perfect new connections too, just at the right time.

You may even experience examples of time taking on a different quality.

Time may stretch and you may begin to tap into 'future memories'. Even time jumps backwards and forwards by a few seconds can also occur.

These are merely examples that you are connecting with a bigger and different reality.

This section of the book may well morph into a bigger book in its own right. These After Words represent an introduction to real world, safe and practical magic.

There is a further caveat to bear in mind when we begin to work magically.

You soon learn that you can have anything you want - the sky is not even the limit. So like a kid in a candy shop, you can overeat and have things that are not good for you. Your new powers can end up controlling you. A true magician is aware of this and does not abuse them. Even though a magician can manifest anything they want, they know that the most powerful way to invoke magic is to take Right Action, Sit Back, Observe and allow the perfect path to Arrive.

Enjoy, experiment and, above all, have fun!

XXIII : Keeping It Simple

Humans have a great ability to over complicate things that are essentially simple.

Sometimes, we can get overtaken by our cleverness, sometimes thinking misguidedly that knowing more 'things' equates to more power. I know this as I am an expert at it!!

When it comes to the Tarot though, I feel that I am a mere novice compared to some people I meet. Despite many attempts, I can't readily even remember (consciously) the linear sequence of the Major Arcana. I would have to refer to a book to 'know' the significance of cards in the Minor Arcana. I don't know how to use complex spreads either.

At first, I saw this as a weakness but more recently I have started to see it as a bit of a blessing. Like the boy in the fairy tale of The Emperor's New Clothes, having fresh eyes gives fresh perspective.

When the detail gets filled in later, it serves then to corroborate hunches and flashes of insight.

The Tarot is awash with Chinese Whispers. The cards have been embellished, tweaked and manipulated down the years. Even the order of Major Arcana has been argued over. They are a magical set of cards though. As well as the original meanings associated with the cards, they seem to accrue the collective new thought associated with them.

This makes it tricky to see the wood from the trees. It also means that any attempt to explain or decipher them, gets added to the collective wisdom which itself could add to the complexity, not simplify it.

So it with all of this in mind that this book and its prequel, Flavours of Thought, were written. Simplicity is the aim. You can judge how well this is achieved. If you are a Tarot expert, forgive my naive approach. If you disagree, let me know and let me know why. I find it interesting that I get great reviews for 'Flavours' from people who know little or nothing about the Tarot. Yet mainly those who use the Tarot for divination occasionally take umbrage. If you rock a boat others may tell you to sit still and be quiet.

The simplest way to use the cards is to experiment. Any magic they invoke is safe and self limiting.

So the first 'spell' to introduce uses just a single card. There is no book to read or spread to learn. It cannot get simpler than that.

So you will need to buy a deck and any deck will do. Think about a current predicament or opportunity. Then, shuffle the cards held face down, and either cut a card or pick the top one. Then leave the deck with that card face up somewhere you will see it during the day, like on your desk or bedside table.

Next you do nothing and just go about your day. The magic from the card will leak out and all you have to do is watch as it kicks in. For example, if you can, when it comes to tricky decisions, try not to make them. Keep a log of coincidences and serendipities.

When you start to see the magic coming into your world, you may have doubts. Is it the cards? Is it you?

We must take care here not to be beguiled and entrapped by the cards. Certainly don't fall into the trap of using them as a prop or 'comfort blanket'. Neither should we allow our ego to inflate thinking we are somehow magical.

The cards by themselves have no intrinsic power. They do though contain considerable potential, embedded in them by their designers.

That potential only gets invoked into the Material Plane by another self-aware consciousness. We need the cards and the cards need us.

So after a week or so of invoking the magic from a single card, it's time to take another step. Again it's not obligatory, just optional, to read up on the Tarot in the mean time. If you feel so minded, go for it. The cards are calling you.

So just split the deck into two piles of the Major and Minor. Then shuffle each deck and cut and turn over a single card from each.

Now you can look at each card and, in the context of the subject you would like insight upon, 'read' a message from the card. You can use the card from the Major Arcana to give you then insight you need. Then use the card from the Minor Arcana to moderate your actions during the day. Once you set your course for that day based on the cards, stick to it. You can always change tack tomorrow.

Again, if you are new to the Tarot, try this for a week before moving on and concocting more powerful and effective spells.

XXIV : Spelling It Out

The Major Arcana consists of 22 cards, or keys, numbered from zero to 21. They start with the zero key of the Fool and end up at 21, The World.

When you buy a new deck, they are normally stacked in order and separately from the Minor Arcana. You can use them as a deck, fan them out or place them in a circle. The Tarot comes from the letters ROTA in a circle after all.

Now I have a pretty good memory but; for some reason, found it really hard to memorise and recall the whole sequence of keys.

When I wrote Flavours of Thought, I found out why. I also sensed intuitively there was a missing key, or Lost Arcana.

When the keys are laid out in the arrangement below, it becomes clear that they are grouped in three rows of seven with the Fool at the top. This grid also shows how I have mapped the Flavours of Thought to each key.

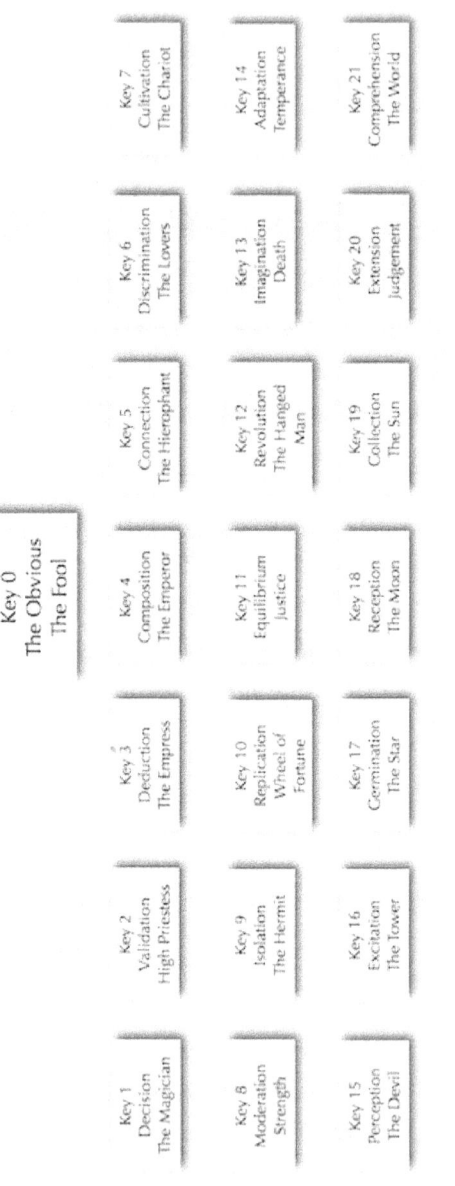

The Pattern of Flavours

Keys 15 to 21 relate to seed ideas in the Archetypal Plane.

Keys 8 to 14 relate to notions in the Creative Plane.

Keys 1 to 7 denote how our conscious mind processes the seed ideas and creative notions by interacting with the Formative Plane.

So this leads us to another simple spread.

Separate the keys from your pile of Major Arcana cards into 1 to 7, 8 to 14 and 15 to 21.

Shuffle each group of seven and lay the out horizontally with the cards face down as shown below.

Place the Fool face up on the right.

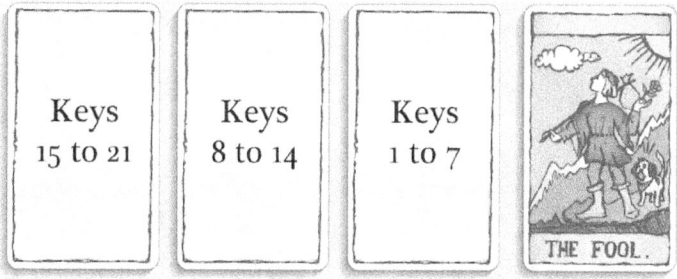

Now think of an issue or opportunity and turn the top card from each group of cards over.

Scanning now from left to right, ending up on the Fool, see if any initial enlightenment comes your way.

Then leave the cards face up for 24 hours some place where you will see them. Let their magic weave and percolate its way from the higher planes, through your unconscious mind into 'reality'.

Congratulations, you have just crafted a spell.

XXV : The Flavours of Thought

I did not plan to write the book Flavours of Thought.

Its genesis came from a chapter of the same name in my book, The Art and Science of Light Bulb Moments. Somewhat ironically, in self-fulfilling fate, I had the light bulb moment while writing that chapter that each Tarot key corresponded to a mode of thought.

Rather than describing each Tarot key pictorially, I have captured its essence as a single word.

These were inspired by Paul Foster Case's book, Key to the Wisdom of Ages, but I also allowed my own intuition to guide me to the word that felt right. I only found out later within this simplicity also lies great power.

This also lead to finding the Lost Arcana.

The Obvious							
Decision	Validation	Deduction	Composition	Connection	Discrimination	Cultivation	Directives
Moderation	Isolation	Replication	Equilibrium	Revolution	Imagination	Adaptation	Unconscious Murmurs
Perception	Excitation	Germination	Reception	Collection	Extension	Comprehension	Ethereal Whispers

With this simplification, it becomes even clearer how the modes of thought fall into three groupings.

The keys 15 to 21 correspond to Higher Self types of thought that I called Ethereal Whispers.

The keys 8 to 14 correspond to modes of thought below our conscious awareness which I called Unconscious Murmurs.

Keys 1 to 7 represent Directives for, and from, the conscious mind.

Thought forms have a natural flow and are seeded in the Archetypal Plane and first enter our auric field as Ethereal Whispers. They percolate into our Unconscious Mind, sometime via our gut and heart minds. Next they sneak into our conscious awareness before we reach a realisation of what is Obvious (the zero key of the Fool which is also Aleph, the Life Breath).

Resist this natural flow and we end up pushing water uphill. Stay in the conscious mind too much with inner dialogue, and you will block both Unconscious Murmurs and Ethereal Whispers.

We can now apply the same technique we used previously to shed light on a situation.

When I do this over the phone, or Skype, with clients, I simply ask them for three numbers (at random) - one between 15 and 21, one between 8 and 14 and one between 1 and 7.

So if I did this now and said 17, 9 and 6. Now, I promise I just made these up without looking and note the image above is not numbered and I had to look at the last section of this guide to work it out. So this flavour combination would correspond to The Star, The Hermit and the Lovers in the Tarot. The corresponding 'flavours' are Germination, Isolation and Discrimination.

The matter which is on my mind as I write this is how best to market my new eCourse called Bending Time.

By ignoring the Tarot correspondences, which are rich but sometimes too awash with symbolism, and using the root thought notions of the 'flavours', the answer has just been given to me on a plate.

Sow lots of seeds - **Germination** - I've done this

Sit back and observe what happens - **Isolation** - like a parent proud of his child, I am not so good at this

Use **Discrimination** and your intuition to know which seeds to water, fertilise and shine light upon - I will do this

Then let go of the outcome and trust that the Universe will lead me to the blindly Obvious.

So now it's your turn.

Choose three numbers at random as above.

Think of something you would like some guidance on.

Work out which flavours correspond to the numbers you selected (look at the numbering of the keys last section in this guide, ensuring you don't cheat)

Then concoct yourself a Recipe for Fresh Thinking.

XXVI : The Essence of the Minor Arcana

You will note that I have hardly mentioned the significance or meaning of any of the cards in the Tarot.

Considering this book is about the Minor Arcana and Flavours of Thought is about the Major Arcana, you may find this strange.

The reasons to take this approach is twofold.

1. I don't know that much about the individual cards

2. I felt that if I got lost in the detail of the individual cards, I wouldn't be able to see the bigger picture

Flavours of Thought distils the essence of each of the Major Arcana into a single word. The description of each flavour of thought, or flought, tells the story of the intelligence behind each key.

The 'anti-flought' describes what happens when we are out of sync with that intelligence. You could see this as an inverted or reversed card in a reading.

The court cards and numbered cards of the Minor Arcana describe a shared language which can be 'spoken' by beings on the four planes. When we pick any card, it stirs up the equivalent 'intelligence', or vibration, or the corresponding plane.

You can see it as opening up a portal between the planes. They represent the *'lingua franca'*, or bridge language, by which beings on each plane can intercommunicate.

For the Minor Arcana, I strongly advocate not engaging our conscious brain and to allow our imagination and intuition (or that of the querent) to come to the fore.

This guide though would feel incomplete without a description of the Minor Arcana. Note this is my personal interpretation based on a number of influences. I encourage you to make up your own.

This is the significance of the Court Cards:

King - our higher self

Queen - our incarnated soul and pattern for this incarnation

Knight - our ego pattern and behaviours

Page - our physical vehicle, our body

The numbered cards have these associations:

10 - completion

9 - the whole

8 - potential

7 - will

6 - options

5 - change

4 - platform

3 - motive force

2 - duality

Ace - seed

So if we were to do an oracular spread and use these interpretations, we might come to a more informed, or influenced, reading. This is why I encourage you to use your own definitions.

By way of example, I just posed this self-fulfilling question.

"How should I best share this resource?"

The cards I picked (or that were picked for me) were:

So the answer I infer from this is:

Ace of Wands: This just represents a seed, and gift, from the Archetypal Plane.

Three of Cups: By continually tapping into the Creative Plane, I will be given all the information I need.

8 of Swords: The seed was just the start of the Formation of almost infinite potential.

6 of Cups: Keep all options wide open.

Only after writing this did I look at the cards (I used the Rider Waite) and the imagery confirmed my interpretation.

So your task now is to do two more oracular spreads on yourself, or someone else.

Do one spread using my definitions of the significance of the cards.

Do another spread using your pre-existing understanding of the cards or, if the cards are new to you, with your own ideas of what the cards mean.

In this way, the baton is passed on and the universal thought pool is increased.

XXVI : The Lost Arcana

I hope this journey around the Tarot has lifted the lid on some of the amazing mysteries it contains. It is so much more than a fortune telling deck.

Elias Levi once said, *"A prisoner devoid of books, had he only a Tarot of which he knew how to make use, could in a few years acquire a universal science, and converse with an unequalled doctrine and inexhaustible eloquence."*

So what if I told you that even with all the gems I've shared with you, there were even more treasures yet to discover about this curious set of cards.

The cards themselves and the spreads are essentially flat. A Flatlander could in theory use and read them.

We though are three dimensional beings and something amazing happens when we see an arrangement of the Tarot in three dimensions.

I came across a glyph called the Cube of Space some years ago. Like the Tarot, at first I didn't understand it and found it overwhelming. With daily use though, it seems the meanings leak into our conscious awareness.

The Cube of Space has the Tarot cards arranged on its faces, edges and some internal, hidden pathways in a very special configuration.

One wet Sunday afternoon, I made a blank cube, replaced the Tarot keys with the corresponding Flavours of Thought and bingo, all was clear.

I had stumbled across the Lost Arcana. I had developed a tool for personal development which, when people go around it, leads to the most amazing transformation.

The Cube of Karma was born. Soon afterwards, people started to wake up!

In the same way our Flatlander goes to the corners of a square to find out where 'Up' might be, when we explore the eight corners of a Cube whilst inside it, we find a new 'Up' ourselves.

In the meantime, enjoy the magic coming into your world.

Glossary

Adytum - a sacred space where secrets can be safely shared

Arcana - a secret of nature sought by alchemists

Archetypal Plane - the 9th dimension or plane of ideas

Clairaudience - the ability to hear sounds and voices from sources not transmitted via the air

Claircogniscence - the ability to know things intuitively that have not been taught

Clairgustatory - the ability to perceive tastes of food and drink you have not consumed

Clairolfactory - the ability to smell odours you have not sniffed

Clairvoyance - the seeing of visions and images that have not passed through your eyeballs

Clairsentience - sensing objects other than through your skin; feeling emotions not linked to your immediate external environment

Creative Plane - the 7th dimension or plane of patterns

Cubelander - one of Us

Dark Energy - this is a force invisible in our three dimensional reality which seems to be pushing the fabric of space apart

Dark Matter - this is the missing 84% or so of the Universe whose existence and properties are inferred from its gravitational effects on the large scale structure of the universe

Descension - the process whereby spirit incarnates in matter

En-darkenment - the opposite of enlightenment and the speciality of some religions and governments

Flatlander - one of Us who never looks Up; or a being who lives a two dimension existence in a world without the dimension of height

Flought - a Flavour of Thought

Formative Plane - the 5th dimension or plane of processes

Guestimate - an estimated guess

Grand Plan - the unseen and unknown point of it all

Inner Oracle - our guide and source of inner-tuition, inner-sight and wisdom

Major Arcana - the 22 keys of the wisdom of ages also known as trumps

Minor Arcana - 56 cards in Four Suits numbered Ace to Ten and each with four Court Cards

Panspermia - organic matter carried to Earth and other planets by cosmic debris such as comets and meteors - some of it exists in free floating form too

Physical Plane - where we live and hang out mostly

Sustend - a combination of sustain and suspend, meaning to 'hold up' and 'hang down'

Tesseract - a four dimensional cube, or hypercube

Thought-full - being full of thoughts percolating down from the Planes of Being

Thought-less - being consumed by inner dialogue and self talk

Uplanders - those of Us who realise their place in the order of things

Veil of Illusion - the 'cloud' that we call 'reality' that has coalesced and densified from humanity being in the state of a consensual dream of our own making

Further Reading

Flatland: A Romance of Many Dimensions, Edwin Abbott

Cosmic Memory, Rudolph Steiner

How to Know the Higher Worlds, Rudolph Steiner

How to Measure the Universe, Kitty Ferguson

Remembering Isis, Madame Blavatsky

The Ancestor's Tale, Richard Dawkins

The Arcturus Probe, Jose Arguelles

The Cerebrum, Emmanuel Swedenborg

The Cube of Space, David Allen Hulse

The Cube of Space, Kevin Townley

The Field, Lynne McTaggart

The Key to the Wisdom of Ages, Paul Foster Case

The Master and his Emissary, Iain McGilchrist

The Science Delusion, Rupert Sheldrake

The Spoken Cabala, Jason Lotterhand

The Tree of Life, Israel Regardie

The Universe in a Nutshell, Stephen Hawkings

Tomography : About the Author

Tom Evans is a 21st century renaissance man. He is an author, poet, healer, karmic mentor and wayseer.

People call him the wizard of light bulb moments.

He discovered he was a natural channel when he wrote a trilogy of fictional life stories called 100 Years of Ermintrude. His non-fiction books explore creativity, what blocks it and the nature of thought.

His latest area of research is called Living Timefully which shows you how to change the speed of time by changing the speed and nature of your thoughts.

He is also the host of the Zone Show, a podcast exploring how we can get in the zone to perform at our peak - and what we do to get back in the zone should the wheels fall off the bus.

He lives in the Surrey Hills with his soul mate and four legged friends who take him for walks when he needs inspiration.

New Magic for a New Era

This is a book of magic.

If you want to know how to bring money, love, good health and luck into your life, it explains how. It is full of practical, real world advice and is brimming with insight and erudition. If you've ever experienced anything out of the ordinary that you can't readily explain, you may well find answers here.

Many personal development books recount how some enlightenment can be gained by encountering and overcoming some adversity or setbacks. This book takes a different approach by exploring the notion that life doesn't have to be intrinsically tough, unless we want it to be.

Visit www.tomevans.co to find out more

AWAKEN YOUR INNER MAGICIAN

www.ingramcontent.com/pod-product-compliance
Lightning Source LLC
Chambersburg PA
CBHW071339080526
44587CB00017B/2897